John Pritchard is Bishop of Oxford and Chairman of the Church of England Board of Education. He was formerly Bishop of Jarrow, Archdeacon of Canterbury and, before that, Warden of Cranmer Hall, Durham. He has served in parishes in Birmingham and Taunton, and has been Diocesan Youth Officer for Bath and Wells diocese. Other books by the author include *The Intercessions Handbook*, *The Second Intercessions Handbook*, *Beginning Again*, *How to Pray*, *Living Easter through the Year*, *How to Explain Your Faith*, *The Life and Work of a Priest* and *Going to Church*. He is married to Wendy and has two married daughters.

For Henry, Cora and future beloved companions

LIVING JESUS

John Pritchard

First published in Great Britain in 2010

Society for Promoting Christian Knowledge
36 Causton Street
London SW1P 4ST
www.spckpublishing.co.uk

British Library Cataloguing-in-Publication Data
A catalogue record for this book is available from the British Library

ISBN 978–0–281–06040–5

3 5 7 9 10 8 6 4 2

Typeset by Graphicraft Ltd, Hong Kong
Printed in Great Britain by Ashford Colour Press

Produced on paper from sustainable forests

Contents

A word at the beginning

I was staying in the fascinating community of Taizé in France where 5,000 young people come each week in the summer to pray, talk, work and share stories. As I wandered around the site I began to notice the variety of messages inscribed on the T-shirts the young people were wearing. The first one I saw said boldly: 'It's all about *me*.' That didn't seem to be quite in the spirit of Taizé, I thought. But then I saw another: 'If found, please return to the pub.' We're still not there, I mused. I became more positive as I began to read the next. 'Devote yourself,' it started hopefully, 'to Heavy Metal,' it ended solemnly.

Finally, coming through the crowd, I saw a T-shirt that said simply: 'Love your enemies.' At last! Here was the authentic spirit of this special place. Here was the echo of Jesus.

We live in a spiritually confused culture. Liam Gallagher of the rock group Oasis once said in an interview,

> I don't pray and I don't go to church but I'm intrigued by it, I dig it. I'm into the idea that there could be a God and aliens and incarnation and some geezer years ago turning water into wine. I don't believe when you die, you die. All the beautiful people who have been and gone – Lennon, Hendrix – they're somewhere else, man. Whether it's here or whether it's there, they're doing some musical thingummyjig. They got to be somewhere else, haven't they?[1]

It's hard to know where to start in deconstructing that statement, but it's not unusual to find 'pick'n'mix' believing. One article in *The Times* on spiritual gurus said,

> In philosophy or spirituality gurus are our cocktail shakers – mixing up a bit of Buddhism, a touch of Kabbalah, some feng shui, a dash of wicca and a pinch of shamanism. So where

does that leave our traditional religious leaders, with their old-fashioned single-brand approach to theisms? Increasingly obsolete.[2]

Religion is being rebranded for the consumer age. There's a mini-industry of guru figures telling us how to take control of our lives with easy slogans: 'There is a power greater than you'; 'Open your heart to love'; 'The past is not the future.' Christian concepts are even slipping back on to the perfume counter: you can spray yourself with 'Purity' and cover your skin with 'Grace'.

However, the answer to profound complexity often lies in profound simplicity. To me, and to millions of others, that profound simplicity is found in the person of Jesus. 'Profound' because the Jesus I shall be exploring in this book is not just one who wants me for a sunbeam. 'Simplicity' because the experience of countless people is that when Jesus is put into the centre of our picture, the rest of life seems to rearrange itself rather satisfactorily.

Note how, even for Liam Gallagher, there in the middle of his observations is a reference to 'some geezer years ago turning water into wine'. Jesus is remarkable for his hold on the popular imagination. A recent survey by the company behind the cult television drama *Primeval* asked which people, now dead, the British would most like to meet. Princess Diana was second and William Shakespeare third, but the clear winner was Jesus Christ.

But who is this Jesus? It turns out that he is deeply elusive. People have tried to co-opt Jesus into their team ever since the stone was rolled away from the tomb, but they never actually manage to recruit him. In the famous words of Albert Schweitzer:

> He comes to us as One unknown, without a name, as of old, by the lakeside, he came to those men who knew him not. He speaks to us in the same words: 'Follow me!' and sets us to the tasks which he has to fulfil for our time. He commands. And to those who obey him, whether they be wise or simple, he will reveal himself in the toils, the conflicts, the sufferings which they shall pass through in his fellowship, and, as an ineffable mystery, they shall learn in their own experience who he is.[3]

It's undoubtedly true that we each have to come to our own understanding of this multi-faceted human being, and yet, through all the countless millions of words spoken and written about Jesus and the three brief years of his ministry, here is a genuine 'man for all seasons'. He has the ability to speak across ages and cultures, across glories and tragedies, across the entire sweep of human emotions, and to do so with a freshness and authenticity that no other person possesses. This book is an attempt to say why.

Here is a man who had no PR machine, no shadowy 'advisers', no lap-top, email or internet. He wrote no book, syndicated no newspaper articles, had no social networking site. He spoke to no more people in his lifetime than would fill the football stadium of a team in the lower reaches of the Championship. But he changed the world more than any person has ever done, and he touches the imagination of more people today than ever before.

The essayist R. W. Emerson said that 'the name of Jesus is not so much written as *ploughed* into the history of the world'. You can't miss him. Even at the trivial level one can see how ubiquitous the name of Jesus has become. When a golfer misses a golf putt it would be very strange if he were to shout 'Winston Churchill!' or when he stubs a toe to yell, 'Mahatma Gandhi!' The name of Jesus is everywhere.

As Philip Yancey points out, 'You can gauge the size of a ship that has passed out of sight by the huge wake it leaves behind,'[4] and you don't get a wake much bigger than Jesus'. This is the basic theme I want to explore in this book. The effect of Jesus on every layer of human experience is quite remarkable, however it is evaluated. He's the magnificent outsider who dominates the Gospels, striding through the pages of the New Testament with glorious freedom. He's the centre point of history, the pivot on which human affairs have so often turned. He's the transforming presence who has turned more lives upside down than anyone could dream of. He's the dynamic personality who has rewritten the rule-book of whole nations, re-framing their laws, their customs, their values, their politics. This Jesus is our partner in prayer and in pain. He's strangely crazy about his Church, and he's been the inspiration of some of the greatest artistic achievements of humankind. Truly, the wake of this apparently minor figure from small-town Palestine has been spectacular in the extreme.

Let's see why.

I want to thank my editor at SPCK, Alison Barr, for believing in this project and not chiding me when it was inevitably late. I also want to thank my loyal chaplain, PA and secretary who patiently keep me on the road. Mainly, as ever, I want to thank my family for showing me the support, interest and encouragement that this jobbing bishop and negligent husband needs when the vapours come over him and he has to start writing. To them goes the credit for getting the book finished; to me goes the responsibility for all the errors of judgement and style.

But I believe in the product. Above all I believe in the subject – the living Jesus, who I try daily to follow.

1

Jesus – a personal obsession

It's time I paid tribute to Sandra. She was my girlfriend in my last year at school. I was brought up in a fine Christian home and going to church was just what you did on Sundays. Through my teenage years the attraction was less about being in the choir and getting paid for weddings, and more about the girls you could meet at the youth club or among the young Sunday School teachers. I believed in God in a vague sort of way but preferred not to get too close. In any case, life held all sorts of vibrant opportunities and wasn't God inclined towards negativity?

But then Sandra began lending me books. They had strange titles, like *The Cross and the Switchblade* and *God's Smuggler*. I read them dutifully but found I was entering a world of Christian faith of which I knew very little. Here were dramatic tales of amazing events, of a God who acted decisively in human affairs, of a relationship with Jesus Christ which wasn't confined to bread and wine at an altar rail but was richly personal and transforming. It was all a bit much for me. I wrote in my list of book reviews (I was that kind of boy) that they were 'very interesting but not very Anglican'. I blush at the memory!

I fear that Sandra and I parted for no better reason than that I wanted a free run at university. Oxford was going to be a new world. But Sandra had made a decisive contribution to my life. She had opened up the possibility that I might be missing something rather crucial about Christianity, that it wasn't essentially something to do with doctrines and good behaviour but rather something to do with a relationship, and in particular, something to do with the living reality of Jesus Christ. The door was opening.

The Jesus I've been offered

As I look back I can see a number of versions of Jesus that I've been offered through the years and the various stages of my journeying. They've all arrived from hidden places in our culture and presented themselves with varying degrees of credibility to my emerging world of ideas and beliefs.

Gentle Jesus

Gentle Jesus is well known in Junior Churches and primary schools all around the Western world. In my own case he was clearly depicted in a picture on my bedroom wall – calm, wise, tall, with blue eyes and fair hair, a strong jaw-line and a strange taste in long white nighties. He seemed to be particularly friendly with little furry animals and birds that should have known better than to hop around on the hands of strangers. But of course this was no Stranger; this was Gentle Jesus, everybody's friend. He was oddly comforting at first but completely remote from my real world. He was epitomized by the words of the Christmas carol: 'Christian children all must be mild, obedient, good as he,' but it has to be said that such a manifesto was hardly attractive to a boy who wanted to play cricket for England and climb Everest. If I got too close to this Jesus, would I have to drink fruit juice at parties and have a cold shower every time I thought of girls? This Jesus wasn't going to go very far in my life.

Judge Jesus

Judge Jesus is alive and well in the dark corners of many minds in traditional Christendom. He particularly afflicts young people in their early teens. He and I got acquainted almost without an introduction. He was just there, watching me with slightly narrowed eyes, not actively intervening but almost certainly disapproving as I struggled through my teenage years. I thought the best way to handle this was to keep my distance and whistle confidently. Gerard Hughes tells of a young married man who lived worthily and simply; he and his wife spent most of their holidays going to Christian conferences. Hughes encouraged him to meditate on the story of the marriage feast at Cana in John 2. He saw tables heaped with food set out beneath a blue sky. The guests were dancing and it was a scene of life and enjoyment. 'Did you see Christ?' Hughes asked. 'Yes,' he said, 'Christ was sitting upright on a straight-backed chair, clothed in a white robe, a staff in his hand, a crown of thorns on his head, looking disapproving.'[1] As Gerard Hughes points out, if he had been asked what image of God he carried in his mind the young man would probably have talked about a God of love, mercy and compassion, but another subconscious image of God was effectively operating in his life, as it does in many devout Christian lives. Judge Jesus is a tyrannical figure who can do great damage if he is allowed to follow us around constantly flourishing a yellow card, getting ready for the Great Day when he can finally send us off the field with a grim red one.

National Trust Jesus

National Trust Jesus is much more benign and really rather well brought up. The great thing about this Jesus is that he's very understated. His churches are a delight to visit occasionally to remind oneself of one's heritage and the virtues of 'the old services'. This Jesus is frozen in time, but usually in a time which never existed. You don't actually need a National Trust card to visit him but you do feel you shouldn't turn up uninvited. Someone once called the Church of England 'the Church that's dying of good taste'. The Jesus I encountered later would almost certainly be respectful of the church-as-National-Trust-property, but he would then most likely go down to the pub and watch the football on Sky. However, in my teens I was on nodding terms with this 'Lilliput Lane' Jesus. He was, after all, innocuous.

Living Jesus

A strange thing happened to me at university. Thanks to my wonderful Christian parents and the preparatory softening-up by Sandra

I was ready to encounter the living Jesus when I was offered an intellectually credible and emotionally satisfying portrait of the man-in-the-middle of the Christian story. Afterwards I wondered how I could have gone so long without seeing that, although I had lots of pieces of the Christian jigsaw, I had never tried to put them together, nor had I realized that I didn't have the big central piece, the one called Jesus. As I thought, listened, read, talked, and finally put that big piece in the centre, so I found that this Jesus stepped off the pages of the New Testament and into my life. It was a Copernican revolution. Instead of having Jesus circling around my sun at a respectably safe distance, now Jesus was the sun and I circled him with varying degrees of trust. I found some words years later which still speak for me. Douglas Webster was a canon of St Paul's and he once spent a dismal winter's day reading Bertrand Russell's book *Why I Am Not a Christian*. He then wrote a brief essay which begins:

> I am a Christian because of Jesus Christ, and for no other conscious reason. I find him unforgettable. I cannot get him out of my system. I do not know how he got there, but I am thankful that he did. I am a Christian because of Jesus Christ, especially because of the way he lived and the way he died, what his death did, and what he did with death in resurrection.

I agree.

Terminator Jesus

Terminator Jesus then made a surprise appearance. It's possible to be so impressed with the new-found energy of faith and the powerful nature of its central figure that we start to believe, and to live as if, 'my God is better than your God'. When we meet opposition we may be tempted to face up to the confrontation and say, 'Wait till I put my tanks on your lawn!' Or even, if defeated, to mutter darkly, 'I'll be back!' Terminator Jesus is an initially attractive figure. He sometimes reappears when the religious right supports international adventures such as the invasion of Iraq.

Here the tanks are chariots of fire leading God's Righteous People to victory. When the television pictures show an 'enemy' target disappearing in a puff of smoke, the Righteous cheer and quote the book of Revelation. But Terminator Jesus doesn't measure up well to the picture of a man on a cross, crying in the darkness. When the gap between these pictures of Jesus becomes too great, one of them has to go. I stuck with the Bible.

Professor Jesus

Professor Jesus is undoubtedly a wise and good man. I met him first at theological college. He took me into the domain of hard, critical thought and wouldn't let me off the intellectual hook. He introduced me to the tools of academic theology and fired my theological curiosity, which has lasted ever since. It has to be said, though, that Professor Jesus sometimes needs to be let out to play and to relax. He certainly needs to tie study together with the life of prayer and practical action. But, then, he's used to that. He's been doing it all his long (pre-existent) life.

Jesus, the Hon. Member for Galilee South

This political Jesus had been lurking in the wings for a while but he emerged more clearly when I went to be a curate in the middle of Birmingham. The human flotsam and jetsam of city life would often drift to the Bull Ring, looking for help. The homeless, the addicted, the desperate – they all had a story to tell, and very often the finger of blame pointed to society and its attitudes as well as to their own personal responsibility. I remember when a night shelter had to close down and people were found dead on the streets. I was there when the IRA pub bombs went off a few hundred yards from our church. I also remember a service in which we took a very long roll of paper and ran it from the pulpit all the way to the west door of our very large church, with an imaginary pencil mark on every inch of its length. How far would that roll of paper need to go so that there was a pencil mark for every hungry person in the world, we asked. To Coventry, London, Dover? The answer was – to Australia, with every inch of the distance representing one desperate human story. These and other seminal experiences convinced me that the message of the kingdom of God was not just one of personal and spiritual significance but one of prime social and political urgency. It was a declaration that the true 'framing story' for the world is one where Jesus is Lord and not Caesar, and the kingdom of God stands as a glowing alternative to the shabby, selfish and oppressive kingdoms of this world. I'm still working this out; I always will be. Perhaps Jesus as the Hon. Member for Galilee South is a bit misleading. I don't believe either Jesus or the contemporary Church can afford to be politically affiliated to a party; Christians have to be affiliated only to Jesus and the kingdom. Nevertheless, there are some who break that rule, on the right and the left. Lord Soper was once asked if he thought it was possible for a Tory to go to heaven. There was a long silence. Eventually Lord Soper said, 'It probably is, but personally I wouldn't want to take such a risk with my immortal soul.'

I hope these various representations of Jesus make the point sufficiently clearly. We can be faced with many depictions of Jesus and we need wisdom to sift the truest, most enlivening pictures of the elusive Stranger who also, amazingly, said to his followers, 'I have called you friends' (John 15.15). But if those are some of the pictures of Jesus that I've been offered, what about the Jesus I've found?

The Jesus I've found

Jesus is much too rich a figure to be bound by any one ecclesiastical tradition. I feel I've benefited from many different dimensions of Jesus shown to me by diverse parts of God's universal Church. You wouldn't expect 2,000 million people all to have the same experience of God or to want to express that faith in the same way. So the truth about Jesus spills over into the many cracked containers we offer him. This is some of what I've found.

Jesus the generous evangelical

John Wesley said that on 24 May 1738 at 8.45, when listening to someone reading Luther's Preface to the Epistle to the Romans at an evening meeting, he felt his heart was 'strangely warmed' and he finally handed his life over in trust to Jesus Christ. Not many people can date their turning to Christ so precisely but many can speak of a time when their faith journey underwent a step-change. I couldn't be precise myself but I know that two weekends at university were seminal and I decided to try living with Jesus Christ as the still point of my turning world.

The evangelicalism I experienced was strong and generous. The important features were the worth and wisdom of the Bible, the centrality of the cross and resurrection as the breakthrough to freedom, the value of making a personal decision to follow Jesus Christ, the importance of daily disciplines of Bible reading and prayer. I remain deeply grateful for these affirmations, all of which I try to live by. I found an evangelicalism that was graceful and welcoming. Doubtless it had its dark side, but I experienced its freedom and light. It was genuinely life-changing. In my case it took me from a career in law to ordination in the Church of England, and I have never regretted that choice for a moment (well, maybe for a moment as I've pulled on a coat for yet another winter evening meeting, but nothing that a day off and a glass of wine couldn't cure). At the centre of this faith has been the compelling figure of Jesus. Evangelicalism keeps on pointing back to this fascinating and deeply attractive person who appeared among us as God's self-portrait, God's first and last Word, and the key-holder to life in abundance. But my journey didn't stop there.

Jesus the earthy catholic

Don't get me wrong with the word 'earthy'. I'm just trying to avoid using the word 'incarnational' too soon. As I journeyed on in ministry as a diocesan youth officer and a vicar in Somerset, I found of course that some of my best friends drew on a more world-centred theology and more sacramental worship. I loved the reverence shown in the Eucharist; something profound was obviously going on there. As one woman stammered out to me, 'That service; it's a ball of fire.' Worship was full of theatre and song, of colour and rich smells, of order and beauty. The ministry that flowed from this deep source was profoundly committed to the welfare of individuals and communities; the bond was intense, never casual. The Church is not a collection of congregations but a holy community, a mystical body. Above all, God's love for the world is incarnated in Jesus, and thus all life and all creation takes on permanent value. Again, Jesus is central and encountered most tellingly in the Eucharist, the constant point of reference for the catholic. I have drawn deeply from this well of faithfulness.

Jesus the Spirit-led 'charismatic'

In the 1970s the 'charismatic movement' was disrupting the established patterns of all our churches. Without so much as a by-your-leave the Spirit seemed to be turning people and churches upside down, like a distant cousin coming into our well-ordered living room and moving all the furniture around, uninvited. But if this was more of the reality of Jesus then I wanted it, so I opened myself to what was known as 'baptism in the Spirit'. And nothing happened. It took me a while to be content that it was God's job to be God. If God wanted to give or withhold that experience then that should be fine by me. God treats us with respect and care; what suits someone else would not suit me. Nevertheless, I was much enriched by the new focus on the work of the living Spirit of Jesus. Worship was loosened up; new, more personal music was released into the Church; people found fresh reality in their well-trodden and perhaps tired paths of faith. Eyes were closed in worship; arms were raised in praise (so much so that the joke went around 'All those who want coffee, put your hands down'). There was much excitement in the air. The intensity has cooled, of course, as the emphasis on the life and work of the Spirit has entered the main bloodstream of the churches. What

God has done is to remind the Church of a neglected truth. God reminded me too.

Jesus the thoughtful liberal

I much regret that the word 'liberal' has become a slur in some quarters of the Church. I've always valued the idea of being open-minded and free to think. Jesus was a liberal in his re-framing of inherited Judaism. He stood free of traditional intellectual and ritual constraints in order to apply the wisdom of God to the world he now inhabited, which was different from the world of the wilderness wanderings in which the law had first been laid down through Moses. The label 'liberal' ought to be worn with courage and a smile. Liberals want to take the world seriously, just as Jesus did. They want to use the best knowledge from the natural and social sciences in order to enrich their understanding of God's world and God's sustaining of it. I won't give up the word 'liberal' without a fight (while turning the other cheek, of course!).

Where the 'centre of gravity' for an evangelical will be *the Bible* and for a catholic, *tradition*, for a liberal that centre of gravity is likely to be *reason* (applied to the Bible and mediated through the tradition). We need all three emphases in rigorous and playful interaction. The observant reader may perhaps have noticed that I have now enlisted Jesus as an Anglican! Those three strands of classic Anglican theological method have served that Church well. It's good to think that Jesus might have felt at home there too.

Brian McLaren says,

> To be a Christian in a generously orthodox way is not to claim to have the truth captured, stuffed and mounted on the wall. It is rather to be in a loving community of people who are seeking the truth on the road of mission, and who have been launched on the quest by Jesus, who, with us, guides us still. Do we have it? Have we taken hold of it? Not fully, not yet, of course not. But we keep seeking. We're finding enough to keep us going. But we're not finished.[2]

The Jesus who has found me

I had been offered various pictures of Jesus through my formative years and I've found a number of other pictures which have made my appreciation of Jesus more multi-layered and rewarding. Nevertheless, I realize that I have also had the experience of being found by Jesus in various ways when I wasn't looking.

The Master of surprise

I used to have a number of paintings and portraits of Jesus which I offered to groups to explore Jesus' two great questions 'Who do people say that I am?' and 'Who do you say that I am?' I then discovered that Bishop Stephen Cottrell has over 1,000 such paintings and portraits of Jesus, from every period and culture. Once I unthinkingly saw Jesus as a European; then I realized he was a Middle Eastern Jew. Then I came across an African Christ and had to stretch my imagination further. Then I saw a Southeast Asian Christ and had to stretch my thinking further still. He represents us all; no race can claim him as its own. Jesus is always bigger than we imagined. I think I understand him, and then he slips through my carefully constructed theological models. I think I know his mind, a Christ-shaped mind, on a contemporary ethical issue, and then I find he's asking me a deeper question and the lines are not so clear. He breaks all my boxes open. He makes mischief with my certainties. He's the Master of surprise.

The Master of disguise

Where is Jesus found today? The question to ask isn't just the old favourite 'What would Jesus do?' but also 'Where would Jesus be?' Would we – do we – recognize him in strange places, and in disguise? In Matthew 25 we are encouraged and dismayed to hear that whatever we do for the least of Jesus' little, lost ones, we do for him. His identification with the needy is pretty comprehensive. Will we recognize him in that strange disguise? It's a discipline, really – the discipline of divine recognition. In Manila a group of

Taizé monks take out food to street people at 3 a.m. Not 2 a.m., because some people who are not really in need would stay up just to get the free food. At 3 a.m. they get the genuine street dwellers. Moreover, they say they are determined to *serve* these people, not just to *distribute* food. The difference is all in the recognition of the Master of disguise, dressed up as a hungry street dweller.

The Master

Jesus gives a deceptively simple call to anyone who will listen. He simply says, 'Follow me.' What could be more straightforward? Jesus invites me to be a follower. Not an expert on first-century Judaism; not a plaster saint; not a member of a secret religious society; just a follower. The difficulty comes in the small print. Dietrich Bonhoeffer, the German theologian executed for participating in one of the plots to assassinate Hitler, once wrote that, 'When Christ calls a man (*sic*), he bids him come and die.'[3] That may be a disincentive! (We'll come back to it later.) But the Master's call is seriously demanding. Here is what one blogger on the internet says about being a Christian:

> The more I try to understand what Jesus was really all about, the more he has the audacity to come into my life and totally screw it up. He makes me think about every dollar I spend – who is benefiting from it and how? He makes me reflect on the kind of car I drive and how it affects God's creation. He challenges me to make my children into risk-taking disciples, instead of neat, middle-class carbon copies of myself. He asks me to go to places where I am uncomfortable, and to invite people into my house when I'd much rather have a quiet night alone. He intrudes on my free time and tells me to invest it in things that matter to him. He tells me that the politics that seemingly support my interests aren't necessarily the ones that support his. Far from being a cosmic Mr Fix-it, Jesus is taking every priority and ambition that I ever held and, without so much as asking, turning it over like he did the tables in the temple.[4]

I guess it's Jesus' prerogative to do all that. Once we've said yes, we have to follow and take the knocks. I still duck and weave to avoid the sharpest challenges to my values and lifestyle. But I'll never shake Jesus off. Indeed, I don't want to. Jesus is a personal obsession.

***

An elderly Pentecostal minister, Dr Lockeridge, was spotted in the crowd at a conference, and as something of an elder statesman, he was asked to come up to the platform and open the conference with a spontaneous prayer. Fortunately it was recorded and this is what he said:

> The Bible says my king is a seven way king:
> He's the king of the Jews – that's a racial king.
> He's the king of Israel – that's a national king.
> He's the king of righteousness.
> He's the king of the ages.
> He's the king of heaven.
> He's the king of glory.
> He's the King of Kings and he's the Lord of Lords.
> That's my king.
> . . . Well I wonder, do you know him?
>
> David said, 'The heavens declare the glory of God and the firmament showeth his handiwork.'
> My king is a sovereign king – no means of measure can define his limitless love.
> No farseeing telescope can bring into visibility the coastline of his shoreless supplies.
> No barrier can hinder him from pouring out his blessings.
> He's enduringly strong.
> He's entirely sincere.
> He's eternally steadfast.
> He's immortally graceful.
> He's imperially powerful.

He's impartially merciful.
. . . Do you know him?

He's the greatest phenomenon that has ever crossed the
  horizon of this world.
He's God's Son.
He's the sinner's Saviour.
He's the centrepiece of civilization.
He stands in the solitude of himself.
He's august and he's unique.
He's unparalleled, he's unprecedented.
He's the loftiest idea in literature.
He's the highest personality in philosophy.
He is the supreme problem in higher criticism.
He's the fundamental doctrine of true theology.
He's the core and necessity for spiritual religion.
He's the miracle of the age, yes, he is.

He's the superlative of everything good that you choose to
  call him.
He's the only one qualified to be an all-sufficient Saviour.
. . . I wonder if you know him today?

He supplies strength for the weak.
He's available for the tempted and the tried.
He sympathizes and he saves.
He strengthens and sustains.
He guards and he guides.
He heals the sick.
He cleanses the lepers.
He forgives sinners.
He discharges debtors.
He delivers the captives.
He defends the feeble.
He blesses the young.
He serves the unfortunate.
He rewards the diligent and

He beautifies the meek.
. . . I wonder if you know him?

Well, this is my king.
He is the king!
He's the key to knowledge.
He's the wellspring of wisdom.
He's the doorway of deliverance.
He's the pathway of peace.
He's the roadway of righteousness.
He's the highway of holiness.
He's the gateway of glory.
. . . Do you know him?

Well, his office is manifold.
His promise is sure.
His life is matchless.
His goodness is limitless.
His mercy is everlasting.
His love never changes.
His word is enough.
His grace is sufficient.
His reign is righteous and
His yoke is easy and his burden is light.

I wish I could describe him to you.
But he's indescribable – Yea! Yea! Yea!
He's indescribable – yes he is! He's God.
He's indescribable.
He's incomprehensible.
He's invincible.
He's irresistible!

Well, you can't get him out of your mind.
You can't get him off of your hand.
You can't outlive him and
You can't live without him.

Well, the Pharisees couldn't stand him, but they found out
    they couldn't stop him.
Pilate couldn't find any fault in him.
The witnesses couldn't get their testimonies to agree.
Herod couldn't kill him.
Death couldn't handle him and
The grave couldn't hold him. Yea!
That's my king!
That's my king! Yea!

And thine is the kingdom and the power and the glory for
    ever and ever and ever and ever
How long is that?
And ever and ever.
And when you get through all the for evers, then Amen!

GOOD GOD ALMIGHTY! AMEN! AMEN!

2

Jesus – the magnificent outsider

About 2,000 years ago there was a man who had royal ancestry but who grew up in very humble surroundings. His life was spent in the service of others, but when he was 30 he and a band of his followers began to wander around the area of the Roman Empire in which they lived. They did this for about three years but their activities began to upset the authorities, so much so that they arrested the young man and crucified him. His name was . . . Spartacus.

Spartacus lived about 70 BC and was the leader of the great slave uprising that led to another brutal Roman repression. Jesus was undoubtedly born in volatile times and there were many like him who were seen in messianic terms as the ones who would save God's holy nation from Roman rule. Yet none of them is more than a footnote in Roman or Jewish history, while Jesus towers over our global narrative in a way no-one else has ever done. What's the difference? Why this astonishing Jesus effect?

Well, first of all, what do we know about Jesus? What would a dossier on Jesus look like?

Jesus of Nazareth: the basic facts

- *Name: Jesus bar-Joseph.* The word *bar* meant 'son of' and Joseph bravely took on this child who he knew was not his own.
- *Date of birth: Possibly spring, 5 BC.* Herod the Great, who reacted so viciously to news of Jesus' birth, had died by the end of March 4 BC. The story of the star seen by the magi may not be as easily dismissed as some have been inclined to do. Chinese

records show there were significant comets in 12, 5 and 4 BC. Only the one in 5 BC was a 'tailed comet', and it was visible for 70 days. Dio Cassius and Josephus both refer to other comets that appeared to 'stop' over cities, possibly when viewed from the north and with the tail of the comet rising vertically from the head, thus giving the stationary appearance. The truth is of course that we can't be sure. It was May or June before the 5 BC comet appeared near Jerusalem, and since the shepherds were in the fields this suggests a spring date, rather than winter.

- *Place of birth: Bethlehem.* Not in a 'stable', which is not mentioned in the Gospels, but most likely in a cave behind a house or inn. Indeed, the word used for inn, *kataluma*, usually refers to the upper guest room of a family house. It may be that there was no room for Mary in the guest room because it was a family house (Joseph's family?) and already full because of visitors for the census. Mary therefore had to go to the warm cave at the back of the house. It's a cave, not a stable, that we see under the Church of the Nativity today.
- *Home town: Nazareth.* Nazareth was a small village of probably no more than 100 people, tucked away in the Galilean hills, and therefore a good place to bring Jesus up quietly after the furore with Herod's soldiers in Bethlehem, which necessitated a quick getaway to Egypt.
- *Occupation: General builder.* Mark 6.3 says that Joseph was a *tekton*, which is usually translated as 'carpenter' but is better translated as 'stonemason' or 'builder'. It may be that Joseph and Jesus commuted daily by a 50-minute walk to Sepphoris, a nearby Gentile city being rebuilt by Herod Antipas at the time, and therefore a place offering plenty of work.
- *Nationality: Jewish.* But Jesus was a Galilean, a man from the north country. Galileans were seen by the sophisticates of Jerusalem as unpredictable and somewhat dangerous provincials.
- *Language: Aramaic, presumably with a northern accent.* Aramaic was the local language but such was the polyglot nature of this mixed Jew–Gentile area that a basic *koine* Greek was used as well, as it was throughout the eastern half of the empire.

- *Appearance: Unknown.* Presumably Jesus would have had a dark Middle Eastern complexion and a beard – far removed from the picture on my childhood bedroom wall.
- *Home address: Capernaum.* Jesus based his ministry in this small but significant border town on the lake. It would have had a customs house and a small garrison – hence the calling of Levi–Matthew and the healing of the centurion's slave. It was on the major trade route, the Via Maris, connecting Mesopotamia and Damascus with the Mediterranean and Egypt, and thus was a strategic place from which a young preacher might hope his message would travel widely.
- *Followers: Fishermen, country boys, zealots, a tax collector, women of some means (Mark 15.41).* Jesus' immediate followers were the 12 disciples, but he had chosen those from a wider group and he also sent out 72 followers on a mission. He was enormously popular with great crowds of ordinary people in Galilee, but when the crunch came, on the cross, those who stood by him were just a few of the women and John.
- *Impact: Changed the world.*

Jesus – the magnificent outsider

Jesus fitted into no ordinary human categories. Teacher – yes, but not with formal rabbinic training. Prophet – yes, but 'more than a prophet'. Political activist – no, but the political implications of his teaching were far-reaching. Revolutionary – not in the normal sense, but his message was outrageously radical. Military leader – certainly not, but many of his zealot followers hoped he would be. Messiah – yes, but not in the way anyone expected. And so on. It's impossible to squeeze Jesus into any of our conventional moulds.

Our primary sources, of course, are the Gospels. These documents have been the subject of more scholarly scrutiny than any other texts in the world's history, and such study has yielded great treasure and great confusion. It has been common for the last 150 years to focus on the construction of the text itself, so various types of textual study have held the field – source criticism, form criticism, linguistic analysis, redaction criticism, literary study and, more recently, sociological and feminist readings of the text. However, new emphases are now emerging under the banner of what are called 'canonic' readings of the text which take it much more at face value and treat it holistically as a text given to the Church for the benefit of both Church and world. The Gospels are again being seen as biography after a long time of being seen as anything but. Even more recently there is a move to give much greater trust to the eyewitness reporting in the Gospels as rich and reliable testimonies of what actually happened.

However we come at these great works, the fact remains that they are works of revolutionary vision. Michael Paul Gallagher writes:

> They are not in the family of philosophy or of theology. They do not analyse or argue. They tell stories that reverse our way of seeing everything. Most of all they tell of a man who walks through these pages with a power no work of literature has ever attained. His is a frightening and yet consoling presence. He disturbs all our comfortable scaffolding. We thought we knew who we were and where we were going. But this Jesus invites us to a deeper joy, something our hearts can recognise, even at a distance. He is in tune with our shy and half-forgotten hungers. He promises us upheaval and yet harmony. He shatters and heals our images. His presence is more like a poetic impact than a neutral truth, and faith is more a drama of the imagination than of thoughts or will or morality.[1]

Perhaps one of the best ways to understand the impact of Jesus, therefore, is to speak of his beauty and the way that beauty has affected millions of Christians and would-be Christians ever since. The effect of Jesus is perhaps experienced more in the response people make in their hearts and imaginations than in their minds and their moral actions. We are used to proclaiming that Jesus is 'the way, and the truth, and the life' (John 14.6), but an appeal to Jesus as *the way* can leave people feeling inadequate because of their knowledge of their own persistent failures. And an appeal to Jesus as *the truth* can leave people cold in an age that no longer values the Enlightenment's loyalty to truth claims. However, an appeal to Jesus as *the life* can excite the imagination because we gladly give our hearts to what is beautiful. As Gerald O'Collins puts it,

> Those people who are beautiful possess an instant appeal. We hope that they are also good and truthful, but it is their beauty that catches and holds our attention. Jesus is the beauty of God in person. When we fall in love with his beauty, we are well on the way to accepting his truth and imitating his goodness.[2]

St Augustine spelt this out in a notable sermon on Psalm 45. He said,

> [Christ] is beautiful in heaven; beautiful on earth; beautiful in the womb; beautiful in his parents' arms; beautiful in his miracles; beautiful under the scourge; beautiful when inviting to life . . . beautiful when laying down his life; beautiful in taking it up again; beautiful on the cross; beautiful in the sepulchre; beautiful in heaven.[3]

Let's look at some of the powerful and beautiful things that Jesus said and did that have captured the hearts of millions and made nations change their course. This is where we see the effect of the living Jesus most vividly.

Jesus the subversive

Some years ago there was a video, mainly for young people, called *The Stranger*. It told the story of a man who came out of nowhere into a Wild West town and refused to wear a badge with a number on it, as every citizen was required to do in order to be assigned to a particular place in society. Worse still, he encouraged others to dispense with their badges too. It drove the sheriff wild because it created social chaos and upset all the norms by which this settled society usually operated. Ultimately, of course, there was only one way out: the Stranger had to be stopped. He was strung up outside the courthouse where everyone could see what happened to people who refused to wear a badge. Of course, there was a sequel . . .

The video was a parable of Jesus' life and the way he subverted the social norms and religious structures of first-century Palestine. The combination of Roman rule and Jewish culture had a profound impact on Palestinian society.[4] The Roman Empire promised peace, security and a pay cheque at the end of the month – unless, of course, you were a slave, in which case you had virtually no rights. And unless you were a small farmer, who couldn't keep up with taxes and had to sell your land to wealthy landowners, and then were in their power. And unless you were a woman, in which case your duty was to marry by the age of 14 and produce a clutch of children. After all, the first prayer in the Synagogue said, 'Blessed art thou, O Lord, who has not made me a woman.'

So all was well in this society unless you were a slave, a small farmer, a woman – oh, or a Samaritan or a Gentile. This unfortunately put you beyond God's blessing, which was intended just for the Jewish people, as God had made abundantly clear in the 40 years of arduous training in the desert and in the 'shock and awe' invasion of Canaan. God was a jealous God. So all was well, unless you were a slave, a small farmer, a woman, a Samaritan or a Gentile – or a tax collector (and so in the pay of the Romans and clearly taking a sizeable rake-off). That made you a hate-figure. And it didn't pay to be a prostitute, either, because you endangered the whole people before God. Even your tithes would not be accepted, so unclean were you to the righteous (= self-righteous). Otherwise all was well – except of course for the unclean, which meant lepers, women with normal or abnormal bodily emissions, women after childbirth, or anyone who had been in contact with a dead body. Oh, and those with mental illness and disabilities.

By the way, there were a few others who had a problem with the settled social order: that is, the 10 per cent of people who failed to show up on the radar at all – day labourers, beggars, outlaws and robbers (sorry about that). So all was well in this ordered imperial–Jewish society unless you were a slave, a small farmer, a woman, a Samaritan, a Gentile, a tax collector, a prostitute, unclean, mentally ill, disabled, a day labourer, a beggar, a robber or an outlaw.

The glorious thing about the Stranger, Jesus, was that he simply refused to play this game. He was constantly criticized by the religious and social authorities for mixing with the wrong sort of people, touching lepers, having meals with tax collectors, meeting and valuing women, playing fast and loose with the Sabbath and the rules on fasting. He was clearly a danger to the system – he just didn't believe in badges. Alison Morgan puts it this way:

> He insisted on treating everyone he met as an individual of equal value, pouring scorn on the hysterical objections of the religious establishment that he was breaking the God given laws of the Jewish people by speaking to the wrong individuals (women, children, outcasts, foreigners, sinners) in the wrong places (at parties, in ordinary people's houses) at the wrong times (on the sabbath) and in the wrong way (without the involvement of the priests).[5]

This Jesus was the one free man in a world of captives.

Terry Eagleton, a Roman Catholic English academic, comes on even more strongly. Indeed, we might want to take issue with him on the detail, but his point is clear. He wrote this:

> Jesus hung out with whores and social outcasts, was remarkably casual about sex, disapproved of the family, urged us to be laid-back about property and possessions, warned his followers that they too would die violently, and insisted that the truth kills and divides as well as liberates. He also cursed self-righteous prigs and deeply alarmed the ruling class.[6]

Such dangerous people are not long for this life.

Jesus the story-teller

Approximately one third of the words of Jesus recorded in the Gospels are in the form of parables. Jesus was simply a great story-teller. Preachers today tend to employ concepts and ideas and almost to apologize for the occasional anecdote lamely slipped in to try to make the sermon connect with life or to keep people awake. Jesus, however, employed stories as often as possible, in vibrant colours and broad brushstrokes. Consider, for example, the images from everyday Galilean life that Jesus used to make his teaching colourful and accessible: wedding clothes and wedding traditions, wineskins, sawdust getting in the eyes, poorly producing trees, bad building foundations, soil, lamps, funerals, ploughing, scorpions, armed robbery, dirty dishes, garden herbs, unmarked graves, sparrows, large barns, ravens and lilies, family disputes, weather forecasting, a donkey falling into a well, mustard seeds, dough, a hen and her chicks, a field and its cows, military strategy, useless salt, lost sheep and mislaid coins.[7]

Jesus was brilliant at using memorable images which served as metaphors, and when those metaphors were extended for a distance they became parables. Much academic ink has been expended on the nature of the parables. It's easier in some ways to say what they are not. They are not systematic illustrations of moral points. They are not single-point stories dressed up in party clothes. They are not allegories designed for point-by-point analogies. Perhaps the best way to describe them is by their effect. Parables act as mental and spiritual hand grenades in the soul, causing us to rethink or reframe some part of life, sometimes quite profoundly. Parables tease and tantalize; they create doubt where there was rigid certainty; they roll around the memory and never quite sit still. Above all they invite response, not just from the head but from the heart and hands as well.

We have become over-familiar perhaps with the junketings of the Prodigal Son, the reckless farming methods of the Sower, the odd thing that happened to a Samaritan on the way to Jericho, the labourers who turned up late to the vineyard, the house built on sand without a thorough survey, and so on. Over-familiarity is a problem, but it's not fatal. If we would linger longer over these tales and pray with them, there is material a-plenty for a lifetime's reflection and refreshment. There are at least 40 of these wonderful word-pictures and it's clear that Jesus was a master at telling these stories, without apology and without explanation. The stories did their own work without the need of plodding through their 'meaning'.

But then again, some of these parables hit powerful people below the belt. They weren't just going to sit and take it. Trouble was brewing . . .

Jesus the teacher

Anyone who has seen the films *Dead Poets Society* or *Mona Lisa Smile* will know how life-changing an inspiring teacher can be. They can shift your perspective and set you up for life. That's clearly what Jesus did in his teaching. People listened to him and came away saying, 'Who is this? He teaches with authority, not like some other people we could mention . . .' He captivated his listeners. They turned out in their thousands, running to catch up with him, eager at whatever cost to hear his glorious word-symphonies and poetic sonatas.

The most obvious gathering together of his teaching is to be found in the Sermon on the Mount in Matthew 5—7. It has to be said that we have admired the Sermon on the Mount more than we have tried to follow it, but nevertheless his provocative statements in that Sermon have tantalized men and women through the centuries just as much as the parables have done. The crazy impossibility of some of his bold assertions and commands have puzzled, attracted and appalled us, but somewhere within us they strike a chord. 'Love your enemies and pray for those who persecute you' (Jesus did just that on the cross); 'If anyone strikes you on the right cheek, turn the other also' (that's caused mayhem in ethical debate ever since); 'Be perfect . . . as your heavenly Father is perfect' (well, he could hardly say: 'Be reasonably good' – but it's a bit daunting nonetheless); 'Everyone who looks at a woman with lust has already committed adultery with her in his heart' (exeunt all men, stage left).

These are stunning little nuggets. 'If anyone wants to . . . take your coat, give your cloak as well' (you cannot be serious); 'If anyone forces you to go one mile, go also the second mile' (a

phrase deep in our culture); 'do not store up for yourselves treasures on earth, but store up for yourselves treasures in heaven' (how
hard we find that one!); 'You cannot serve God and wealth' (game,
set and match); 'Do not judge . . . First take the log out of your
own eye' (almost universally ignored); 'Ask, and it will be given
you; search, and you will find' (a promise claimed a million times
a day in prayer); 'Not everyone who says to me "Lord, Lord" will
enter the kingdom of heaven, but only one who does the will of
my Father' (oh dear . . .).

What has been the effect of all these extraordinary lines? Some
have seen the demands as deliberate hyperbole to emphasize the
need to aim higher. Some have gone a stage further and seen it
as a ploy to make us realize we depend utterly on grace, so impossible is the standard set before us. Others have seen the Sermon
as a statement of a new ethic for a new time, a new law to replace
the old Mosaic law, and yet others have seen it as a call of aspir-
ation so that our personal spiritual and moral intentions are
aligned with the purposes of the kingdom of God.

I warm to the view of Robert Farrer Capon who, in his book
The Mystery of Christ – And Why We Don't Get It, says simply,
'We're so used to standing on our heads that when God shows
up, we think he's the one who's upside down.'[8] Tom Wright sees
it similarly. He says,

> Jesus is not suggesting that these are simply timeless truths
> about the way the world is, about human behaviour. If he
> was saying that, he was wrong. Mourners often go uncom-
> forted, the meek don't inherit the earth, those who long for
> justice frequently take that longing to the grave. This new
> Kingdom is an upside-down world, or perhaps a right-way-
> up world; *and Jesus is saying that with his work it's starting
> to come true.* This is an announcement, not a philosophical
> analysis of the world. It's about something that's starting to
> happen, not about a general truth of life.[9]

In the Sermon on the Mount Jesus is saying that he is taking
control and starting to put things the right way up at last. He is

saying: 'You are entering a new world, the alternative world of the kingdom, and you will be blessed with a true connection to God and to being human together.'

The crispest and most provocative part of that Sermon is what we know as the Beatitudes. They have affected millions of people in more profound ways than we could imagine. They have all the strangeness and appeal of the rest of the Sermon and it's important that we don't spiritualize them out of their context. They refer in large part to the poor or *anawim* of God, the socially and economically deprived, who will find that in the new economy of the kingdom they will be blessed beyond measure and beyond expectation. Nevertheless, the Beatitudes have also spoken to ordinary Christians about some kind of call to 'let go':

Blessed are the poor in spirit, for theirs is the kingdom of heaven. Letting go of our need to be somebody.
Blessed are those who mourn, for they will be comforted. Letting go of our pain.
Blessed are the meek, for they will inherit the earth. Letting go of our need to be right.
Blessed are those who hunger and thirst for righteousness, for they will be filled. Letting go of our concern for ourselves.
Blessed are the merciful, for they will receive mercy. Letting go of our need for revenge.
Blessed are the pure in heart, for they shall see God. Letting go of our need to look good.
Blessed are the peace-makers, for they will be called children of God. Letting go of our need to win.
Blessed are those who are persecuted for righteousness sake, for theirs is the kingdom of heaven. Letting go of our 'safety first' approach to life.

Countless followers of the living Jesus have found that these truths resonate with their experience.

Two final comments on the extraordinary teaching of Jesus. First, the Chief Rabbi, Jonathan Sacks, believes that the three most significant words in the New Testament are 'But I say . . .' He says there is no evidence of any rabbi saying anything like that; they always quoted the authority of Scripture (Torah) and the classic interpreters (Talmud). Jesus took the responsibility of deeper interpretation on himself. 'You have heard it said . . . , but I say . . .' This was the basis of Jesus' authority; the Jewish people had heard nothing like it.

The other comment is a succinct summing up of the teaching of Jesus by Herbert McCabe: 'If you don't love, you're dead. And if you do, they'll kill you.'[10] This teaching of Jesus, combined with his actions, made following him a distinctly dangerous road to take.

Jesus the healer and miracle-worker

You can't separate out the healing stories from the 'real' life of Jesus. In Mark's Gospel, nearly half of the account of Jesus' public life is concerned with miracles. They were the deeds of power which anticipated the full rule of God which was now on its way. Mark shows Jesus wanting to keep these miracles quiet (the messianic secret), and John describes the miracles as 'signs' of the divine truth in Jesus, clues to his true identity. But it seems to have been inevitable that the life-giving love of Jesus would 'leak out' of him and do remarkable things.

Everyone who has thought about the Gospels has their own view of what was going on in these miracle stories. For some, there is no problem because once you have conceded the great miracle of the incarnation of God in a human life, then everything is possible. In Jesus the love of God was at full stretch and so the possibilities multiplied. For others there is no possibility of the regularities of nature being suspended by anyone; the stories have been 'read back' into the life of Jesus from the vantage point of a post-resurrection faith. Others again find they make an *ad hoc* distinction between the miracles of healing and the much harder nature miracles (walking on water, stilling the storm, turning water into wine, feeding the 5,000).

The important points are surely these. First, the meaning of the miracles is more important than their historicity. They pointed towards God's creative rule (the kingdom) breaking in to reset the world's compass to its true north. Second, to rule out miracle on the *a priori* grounds that nature is a closed system and miracles simply cannot occur is both poor logic and, increasingly, poor science, because science is prepared to allow for the unexpected and downright extraordinary. Physicists in particular are used to dealing with uncertainty. Third, perhaps miracles are not breaches of natural law so much as the natural law of a deeper order of reality, a summoning of those reserves of nature which underlie common experience. Thus Jesus performed his miracles not as God but as man, but man who, as Austin Farrer put it,

> experimented with Omnipotence, and let it find its own limits. Maybe there were things that Divine Love would not do because God loves the order of the world as well as the happiness of man (*sic*). But Jesus had nothing to fear – he would be shown as he went; he would know in himself what it pleased Almighty Love to do.[11]

And what Jesus did then, the living Christ seems sometimes to do now.

Inevitably the effect of the miracles has been to focus attention on their historical factuality, just as Jesus feared. (He was more concerned about their meaning as signs of the kingdom.) More important is the passion and energy behind the whole of Jesus' ministry, of which the miracles are just a part – though an inevitable one, given who Jesus was. David Day puts it like this:

> In the gospels we see a battle against the powers of evil and all that that phrase includes – disease, decay, death, slavery to destructive forces, prejudice, hardness of heart. Jesus systematically waged war on everything which destroyed, distorted, cramped and enslaved human life. Whenever

Jesus finds evil in his ministry he opposes it. The movement of his life, its driving force and direction is *against* evil and *for* health, freedom, forgiveness, wholeness and fullness of life.[12]

So Jesus was bound to be a healer, and Christians have been bound to be involved in founding hospitals, hospices and healing ministries ever since.

Jesus the visionary

The point we have reached allows us to see that everything Jesus said and did was pointing to an alternative reality which he called the kingdom of God. The kingdom was central to his life and thought, and we can see how distinctive it was to him by the scarcity of references to the kingdom in subsequent New Testament literature. Kingdom-talk was quite definitely Jesus' own way of presenting his central vision.

Jesus didn't come with a manifesto for political reform. He didn't come with a blueprint for the Church. He didn't come to lay out a new ethical system. He came with a vision of the kingdom and he presented it as an alternative to the prevailing social and religious reality. 'He is announcing a different order, with a different value system and a different set of rewards – for all the wrong people.'[13] What Jesus presented was not a coherent platform for a religious campaign. He offered a set of metaphors, images and stories to challenge his listeners at the deepest level of the imagination, where visions grow, dreams are cooked slowly, and courage matures into action.

'Let anyone with ears, listen!' said Jesus.

The invitation is still on the table.

Jesus the dying and rising God

Where was all this heading? The subversive, story-telling, teaching, healing, visionary Jesus – were the lines coming together somewhere, like some tragic experiment in perspective? The inevitable point of convergence was that dark cross against a blood-red sky. A life lived that close to the light was bound to get burnt. Humankind can't stand either too much reality or too much goodness. We have to destroy that which shows us up so painfully. Through sheer integrity and by keeping the spotlight clearly on the alternative kingdom on which he had cut the ribbon, Jesus' life was time-limited from an early stage – already in Mark 3 we find the Pharisees conspiring with the collaborating Herodians to destroy Jesus. You can't take on the imperial, religious, economic and aristocratic authorities all in one go and expect a happy ending.

The method of killing Jesus was far from unique and was hideously cruel. It had the naked victim covered in sweat and blood, moaning and sobbing, gasping for the occasional breath, falling back as his lungs filled with liquid, drowning and dying over days, usually, and then the rotting remains attended to by scavenging crows, vultures, feral dogs and a cloud of flies. Jesus died more quickly than that, but how was this sight one that cohered with the glorious vision he had opened up to his followers in Galilee? What can one say on Good Friday?

David Scott, a priest poet, wrote:

> The answer is, I think, that you don't say very much, although it does help to keep telling the story. That's what the evangelists did. And you can wonder. And some days you say: 'My God!' and other days you just hope the image of the crucifixion will burn into your own body, so that you will be like him. Your thoughts however won't have words every day, just silences and sighs too deep for words, and one day you will even find yourself saying: 'He did that for me,' and even: 'He did that for my enemy.'[14]

The fury of the cross is hard to contemplate, but Christians believe that God himself was there in that lonely, forked figure, and that he was taking on himself the massive attack of the forces of evil – and defeating them, although the battle was appalling. This is the crucified God absorbing that evil; that's what makes sense of this sorry spectacle that has nevertheless towered over history for 2,000 years. This is our God, the Servant King.

And yet, and yet, God is never ultimately defeated; that would be a contradiction in terms. Love rises again because love has the first and last word in a world created by and with Love. In both creation and redemption it's Love Unlimited that's at work. The tomb was empty; the bird had flown; a new creation was burning through the morning mist.

I've never seen a depiction of the resurrection in art, film or theatre that rises far above the banal or the kitsch, but how do you represent in two dimensions something that exists in 20?

There's a scene in Mel Gibson's bloody *tour de force, The Passion of the Christ,* when Jesus falls on the way to the cross and Mary his mother rushes to him as she used to when he fell over in the sunny streets of Nazareth when he was a child. Down there in the dirt, the blood, the sweat and the ignominy Jesus manages to gasp to Mary: 'See, Mother, how I make all things new.'

It's crazy but true: 'I make all things new.' He has done; he is doing; and he will do.

Following Jesus

So what are we to do with this magnificent outsider? The answer for millions of people is simple: follow him. After all, as Rob Bell says:

Everybody is following somebody. Everybody has faith in something and somebody. We are all believers. As a Christian, I am simply trying to orient myself around living a particular kind of way . . . And I think that the way of Jesus is the best possible way to live. This isn't irrational or primitive or blind faith. It is merely being honest that we are all living a 'way'. I'm convinced being generous is a better way to live. I'm convinced forgiving people and not carrying around bitterness is a better way to live. I'm convinced having compassion is a better way to live. I'm convinced pursuing peace in every situation is a better way to live. I'm convinced listening to the wisdom of others is a better way to live. I'm convinced being honest with people is a better way to live. This way of thinking isn't weird or strange; it is simply acknowledging that everybody follows somebody, and I'm trying to follow Jesus.[15]

Me too! And I know I can't do it by myself. I need, somehow, the strength of Jesus himself to live like that. Fortunately, God has thought of that too. We are given the Spirit of Jesus within us to supply the grace and energy we need to begin living his 'way'. Without the indwelling Christ the best we could do would be to move stiffly and awkwardly through life like robots on autopilot. To have the suppleness and generosity of Christ we need his presence within. The heart of Christian living is not about beliefs and behaviour; it's about union with Christ. 'Christ in you – the hope of glory' (Col. 1.27).

Occasionally you come across lives that hum with the grace and beauty of Jesus, and it's a humbling experience. Their secret is that they've lived with Jesus for a long time.

3

Jesus – centre point of history

H. G. Wells once wrote, 'I am a historian. I am not a believer. But I must confess, as a historian, this penniless preacher from Galilee is irrevocably the very centre of history. Jesus Christ is easily the most dominant figure in all history.' In a similar vein, historian Kenneth Scott Latourette wrote, 'As the centuries pass, the evidence is accumulating that, measured by his effect on history, Jesus is the most influential life ever lived on this planet.' In only slightly more cautious terms, theologian Hans Kung wrote,

> After the fall of so many gods in this century, this person, broken at the hands of his opponents and constantly betrayed through the ages by his adherents, is obviously still for innumerable people the most moving figure in the long history of mankind (*sic*).[1]

This is the claim I want to explore in this chapter – that Jesus is the hinge on which history turns. Even our dates are reckoned in years before or after Christ. And yet the European Commission in its wisdom has come up with a form of constitution, the preamble of which makes no acknowledgement of the complete dependence of European culture on Christianity. It presumes that European cultural history moved straight from Graeco-Roman foundations to the present day. The most cursory glance at European history, political structures, citizenship, science, art, literature, music, poetry, theatre and so on, discloses overwhelming evidence that the figure of Jesus Christ has been at the centre of European thought.

How is it that the Christian gospel has become merely a painting on the wall, familiar but almost unrecognized, when in fact it has been the prime motivator of the West's political, social and cultural energy? Perhaps because the painting has been allowed by the Church to become dulled and discoloured, so that although the outline of the figures can be seen, the vibrant colours have all but disappeared. The Church needs an expert picture restorer to clean the grime away from the varnished surface. Fortunately that's exactly what the Church has in the Holy Spirit, a wise, skilled and experienced restorer of all that is precious. If only the Church let the Spirit in more often!

Early days

First we need to see how this story about an untrained artisan and travelling teacher, astonishing as it was, could come to hold such a key place in the world's life that H. G. Wells could say that Jesus is the centre of history. After all, things did not augur well at the start. Consider this spoof memorandum from the firm 'Jordan Management Consultants' to Jesus, the would-be prophet at 'Joseph and Son, General Builders, Nazareth':

Dear Sir:

Thank you for submitting the CVs of the 12 men you are considering for management positions in your new organization. All of them have taken our battery of tests and undergone personal interviews with our psychologist and vocational aptitude consultant. It is our opinion that most of your nominees are lacking in appropriate background, education and aptitude for the type of enterprise you are undertaking. Simon Peter is emotionally unstable and given to fits of temper. Andrew has no qualities of leadership. The two brothers, James and John, place personal interest above company loyalty. Thomas demonstrates a questioning mind that would tend to undermine morale. We feel it is our duty to tell you that Matthew has been blacklisted by the Jerusalem Better Business Bureau for possible fraud. James, son of Alphaeus, and Thaddeus both show radical leanings and score highly on the manic-depressive scale. None of them seem inclined to team work.

There is, however, one candidate who shows potential. He is a man of ability and resourcefulness, has a keen business mind and is well connected. He is motivated, ambitious and can take responsibility. We recommend Judas Iscariot as your deputy and assistant and feel sure he would be an asset to your organization. All the details are in the enclosed dossier.

We wish you every success in your new venture.

This was the team (bar one) who Jesus had to rely on to start the ball rolling after he had finally left them to it. They might have been spooked by the responsibility, but nevertheless it's likely that within 50 years of Jesus' death nearly 30 per cent of the world's population had been exposed to the gospel, and with the conversion of Constantine in the early fourth century the whole Roman Empire was officially Christian. Jesus was already at the centre of the known world. Was any movement so effective?

This staggering success came in large part from the overwhelming enthusiasm of those transformed disciples. Every vicar in England would love to have a set of such turbo-charged followers of Jesus. Broadcaster Libby Purves tells this story:

Matthew Parris often proclaims his unbelief but once, looking at what Christianity preaches, he said he couldn't understand how people who do believe all this stuff somehow manage to live their lives exactly as he does. If he did believe it, he says, he would have to think of nothing else, to live no other way, and to proclaim the good news day and night. Which [as she wryly observes] is more or less what Christians were told to do 2000 years ago.[2]

Such complete devotion from the first disciples must have come from being gripped by an irresistible conviction that Jesus was the centre-piece who gave meaning to the whole of life. The truly astonishing thing is that these down-to-earth, unlikely heroes came to see their friend and travelling companion of those three exciting years as Lord of history and Son of God. They were pretty amazed too, but their experience drove them there.

> We declare to you what was from the beginning, what we have heard [honest!], what we have seen with our eyes [our own eyes!], what we have looked at and touched with our hands [these hands here!], concerning the word of life – this life was revealed, and we have seen it [believe me!] and testify to it.   (1 John 1.1)

You can smell the amazement rising from the page.

They were forced to this conclusion from what Jesus said and did (see the previous chapter), and because of some of his especially significant actions, such as claiming to be able to rewrite Torah, to forgive sins (only God could do that) and to be opening the door to the new age to come. The categories that properly applied to God alone seemed to fit Jesus like a glove. And so it was that within a few decades of his life, death and new life a whole host of the most exalted images were being applied to this Jesus. One calculation numbers over 200 titles and images given to a man who many eyewitnesses had only recently been talking to about blisters and barbecues and whose turn it was to do the washing up.

Try these titles: good shepherd, true vine, tree of life, living water, bread of life, rock of ages, mighty God, root of David, Immanuel, day star, first born of the dead, wisdom of God, horn of salvation, lion of Judah, new Adam, sun of righteousness, desire of nations, lamb of God, cornerstone, brightness of the Father's glory, Son of God, and so on. The list is breathtaking, both in extent and in the intensity of the images. Is there anyone you have ever met to whom you would apply any one of those titles?

By the beginning of the fourth century the whole Roman Empire had officially signed up to these beliefs.

Jesus in time

It is commonly argued that Jesus, and the Christianity that followed him, changed our view of time and history. Before him time tended, in Greek and Roman thought, to be seen as circular. Plato saw time as giving order and shape to the world by endowing life with a regular, repeating structure of days, seasons and years. Aristotle connected time not only with the human cycle of life and death but with the circular movement of the planets. This circular view of time was seen as obvious, so when Christians came along with a linear understanding of time it was a radical move in philosophical thinking. Christians saw time as moving in one direction only, towards a final conclusion in the kingdom of God. Augustine argued that circular views of time were miserable and prevented anything new, whereas a Christian understanding of time allowed for change, development, renewal and growth. This linear understanding of time has become the dominant model with which people now live, although it has been corrupted into a secular belief in the inevitability of progress, which any reading of history with its repeated brutal and dreadful events ought quickly to dispel. Christianity suggests we can prepare the raw materials for the kingdom but that we can't build it ourselves; it's in the hands of God. Our journey to the kingdom may be uni-directional but it isn't a smooth path of progress. There are battles all the way along the road.

Nevertheless, many Christian thinkers have wanted to encourage the belief that history can demonstrate the progress of human society towards a perfect future. The nineteenth-century German philosopher Hegel argued that 'history was the outworking of logical social processes that would bring about the Kingdom of heaven on earth'.[3] He saw time as having three ages: the age of the Father (before Jesus' birth), the age of the Son (when Jesus showed us how to live well together) and the age of the Spirit (in which those ideas would be worked out and the kingdom would be realized). This thinking influenced Karl Marx, as it also did generations of actively committed Christians seeking social justice. What is required is not any diminution in that passion for justice but rather a little more theological humility in evaluating the significance of the results. The kingdom is always God's gift, not our construction.

However, there was another joker in the Christian pack along-side this radical idea of linear time, and that was the idea of *kairos* time, meaning time as 'opportunity' or 'the right time'. Jesus saw his coming and the coming of the kingdom as kairos moments. Paul saw Jesus' death and resurrection as the major kairos events, as would be the second coming of Christ at the 'end of time'. *Kairos* is an understanding of time distinct from *chronos*, which is the mere passage of events. It is, to use the image of Hugh Rayment-Pickard, a way of seeing time 'not so much as a line as a pattern of dots, where each dot represents a unique historical opportunity'.[4] In fact we all probably see our lives in this way. When I tell my story to anyone I don't give them a dull chronology of everything I've ever done; rather, I pick out the significant moments (the kairos moments) which give my story colour, contour and texture.

It is in this kairos sense that we can think of Jesus as the centre of history. He was in himself the ultimate kairos moment. The eruption of Jesus into history is the definitive intervention of God. It was the time when the divine lightning struck the earth, when the eternal Word became flesh. It was an unrepeatable, time-changing particularity. The divine Author had appeared on stage. To change the image, it was the time when the weak, intermittent signal to which men and women had borne witness through the centuries became the loud, clear signal which said that God was among us, and around him everything else would ultimately cohere (Eph. 1.10).

Jesus and cultural context

For Jesus to be seen as central to the world's history we have to see how the faith formed around him has fared in different cultural and political contexts. One of the simplest and most flexible definitions of culture is provided by Lesslie Newbigin, who wrote that a culture is 'the sum total of ways of living developed by a group of human beings and handed on from generation to generation'. He also defines gospel as 'the announcement that in the series of events that have their centre in the life, ministry, death and resurrection of Jesus Christ something has happened that alters the total human situation and must therefore call into question every human culture'.[5]

The history of the West has been in large part the story of how the Christian gospel has negotiated its place in different cultural contexts, sometimes by assimilating the gospel into the surrounding culture, and sometimes by standing over against it. For example, in the Middle Ages the assimilation was so far advanced one could say that an entire Christian culture was created; society itself was Christian and the work of the Church was no longer in mission but in education, church-building, wealth creation and political intrigue. This was probably not what Jesus had in mind.

Later in the Middle Ages there was a gospel-based reaction against this through the creation of religious communities such as those founded by Francis, dedicated to a radical renewal of Christian mission through poverty and acts of compassion, and Dominic, who made teaching and learning exciting and converting. In the Renaissance the Church was again led into assimilation as it championed the arts and enjoyed the privilege of being at the heart of society, but soon after came the fierce response known as the Reformation, where the gospel assurance that only undeserved grace could lead to salvation was set against a self-congratulatory and self-indulgent culture.

In the seventeenth-century 'age of reason' the Church made heavy weather of handling the rise of modern science but was socially complacent as well. It wasn't until the eighteenth-century revivals which struck Germany through the Moravians, the UK through the Wesleys and America through the preacher Jonathan Edwards that a refreshed faith was brought to bear both on the Church and on social ills, processes which continued into the nineteenth century, when major ecclesial renewals and social reforms changed the face of the UK and Europe.

It was in the twentieth century that the centrality of Jesus Christ came under the most intense attack when the aggressive ideologies of Nazism and Communism made a bid for centre-stage. Hitler and Stalin between them accounted for more than 100 million deaths in their terrible political and military projects; other regimes such as those of Mao Tse Tung and Pol Pot accounted for millions more. It cannot be said that the faith around Jesus Christ always emerged from these encounters crystal clean, but it is nevertheless the case that the moral bankruptcy of these two huge ideologies led to their proper demise, while Christianity continued to grow, embracing now a third of the world's population. Even in China it is said that there are 10,000 new Christians every day.

There is at least a *prima facie* case, therefore, for saying that Jesus remains, as H. G. Wells said, the 'centre of history'. The story is not always a noble one but the Christian faith is still the framing narrative that holds more people together than any other.

But what about the other story that could be told?

The dark story of Christianity

I was leaning over the side of the ship with a huge party of school students on board. I was chaplain to this schools cruise and a thoughtful teacher from a school in Somerset came up and leaned over the rail with me. 'Tell me,' he said, 'why has Christianity been responsible for so many terrible things in human history? Why has it been so demonic?' I was young and idealistic, and I hadn't previously experienced such a bold attack on the faith that I had found so pure, life-giving and true. But it was one of those moments of disclosure about a conviction that is increasingly voiced, as a more aggressive atheism has been let off the leash.

There is no denying the dark seam that has run through Christian history. I need only cite the Crusades, the Inquisition, Northern Ireland and Bosnia, as well as support for racism in the American south and in South Africa. The story of the colonization of South America, Africa and elsewhere can hardly fill Europeans with pride – and Christians were complicit in those actions. And what about the Church not adequately naming the demon in Nazism? Or a 'Christian country' dropping a bomb on Hiroshima with a death toll of 80,000? All of this is hardly the way Christians would want Jesus to be the centre point of history.

Most of the situations cited were the result of complex interactions of political, social and economic factors as well as religious ones. Nor should we too easily bring the beliefs and behaviours of the past to the bar of the present. The gospel is often like a slow-burning fuse: it takes a long time to explode. This was what happened when eventually slavery was recognized as totally unacceptable, or when women began to get their respected place in society. Moreover, religion is often the fall-guy for blind nationalism, when religion is the label but not what's in the tin.

When Jonathan Swift wrote that 'we have just enough religion to make us hate, but not enough to make us love one another' he pretty well named the problem. We need healthy religion, not its unhealthy cousin, and we need religions that have built-in mechanisms for self-criticism. One day a mother brought her child to see Mahatma Gandhi because the child was addicted to sweets and the mother wanted Gandhi to persuade the little girl to exercise restraint. Gandhi asked the mother to take the little girl away but to come back in three weeks. She did that and Gandhi persuaded the child to cut back on sweets. The mother was grateful but then asked Gandhi, 'Why, Gandhiji, did you not say this to the girl three weeks ago?' Gandhi replied, 'Because three weeks ago I too was addicted to sweets.'[6] As Jesus would say to us, we need to take the plank out of our own eye before we remove the speck out of another person's eye. Christianity has much to repent of too.

The centre point of history?

When I was younger I would have defended H. G. Wells' statement as a matter of fact. Now I think I would defend it more as a matter of faith. My confidence in the ultimacy of Jesus Christ leads me to say that for me Jesus is indeed the still point of this turning world. That Jesus really is the hinge of history. I have to recognize objectively, however, that in a postmodern reading of history no person or event or political ideology could claim supreme significance. Postmoderns don't accept any 'meta-narrative';

all meanings are constructed. Nevertheless, it would be hard for any other person to come nearer to that claim of centrality than Jesus. Who else could you put forward?

Jesus remains unassailable, I suggest – God's Word to us from the centre of history.

Jesus – the centre of our personal history

Whatever we make of that suggestion, however, there is another sense in which Jesus is 'the centre', and that's the centre of the personal history of millions of followers. The experience I had at university, which I previously described as a kind of Copernican revolution, was one where Christ, in a way that's hard to describe, 'took up residence' at the centre of my life and decision-making. He simply became the central vision, the guiding star. As I've gone on in the Christian journey I've sometimes lost the joyful simplicity of that homecoming, by which I came home to God and he came home to me. I needed to be reminded of it once when I went on retreat and an ancient Jesuit priest (modelled closely, I thought, on Bilbo Baggins) advised me to 'let Christ ease his way into your life – so that it's no longer you who live but Christ who lives in you'. He was quoting Galatians 2.20 but he was spot on. I love the idea of Christ 'easing' his way into my life; it's gentle, only done with permission, and expresses perfectly the relationship I seek with the living Jesus.

Here we've come to the heart of what it is to be a Christian disciple. A Christian is not someone who tries hard, goes to church a lot and has the truth captured, boxed and safely on a shelf. A Christian is someone who has put his or her life together with Christ, in a relationship of trust. The New Testament has a number of images of this: *knowing* Christ (Phil. 3.10), *receiving* Christ (Rev. 3.20), *coming to* Christ (John 7.37), being *in* Christ (2 Cor. 5.17), Christ living *in us* (Gal. 2.20) and so on. The description we use doesn't matter so much as the reality we're trying to express – that we've come together with Christ in a relationship of trustful union and effective following.

I once sponsored a man for ordination and asked him to write about his Christian journey. He said:

> If being a Christian means giving your assent to the basic tenets of the Christian faith, then I became a Christian at the tender age of six. If it means having received the forgiveness of sins through Jesus Christ and his death and resurrection, then I was converted at age twelve. If it means being baptised and giving a public confession of faith, then I received the gift of grace at age fourteen. If being a Christian means trusting God to guide you through life, then I was twenty before I had faith at all. If it means being confirmed and receiving the blessing and the laying on of hands from an ordained bishop, then I saw the light a year and a half ago in the cathedral. This may sound flippant, but the point I want to make is this: I started my journey of faith in Sunday School before my fourth birthday, and yet now, at the mature age of forty, I still need to turn to Christ every day as if it was for the first time.

Here was a man who understood the complex simplicity of faith and who knew, for all his intellectual ability, that at heart faith is a matter of turning afresh to Christ every day and seeking to put him at the centre.

This is where the history of the world, and our own personal history, come together. It's Christ who makes sense of them both.

4

Jesus – changing the rules

I once received a card with the caption, 'I tried to change the world – but I couldn't find a baby-sitter.' It's the dream of many of us, that we can truly make a difference to this tired old world, but there are one or two obstacles in our way. We've seen the answers in this beguiling paperback we've just read, or we've had a vision in the night and the way is clear. The problem is that life keeps intervening.

To bring about radical change in such a complex global environment as we live in, we need a huge lever. I was listening to Jonathon Porritt speaking about the challenge of global warming and he spoke plainly.

> We need new technologies, and smart, sustainable consumption, and the ability to take some pain as we change our lifestyles, but what we need most of all is a powerful enough motivator for people to be prepared to change, and that can only come from the world's great religions.

The lever is heavy and rusty; but only something that gets to the deepest springs of belief can cause us to change our ways.

Foremost among those change-makers in human society in the past has been Jesus. Tim Butcher's book *Blood River*[1] tells the story of his passage through the Democratic Republic of the Congo, following the steps of Henry Morton Stanley. It's a sad tale of the degradation of a culture and the disappearance of most signs of progress, but the writer keeps coming across two types of survivor organizations still working for the people: the United Nations and the missionaries. Who is left when the media has moved on from the world's latest disaster zones? The answer is – Christians. Where things are humanly at their darkest, only those with an indestructible light can survive.

The Church of God, in trying to be faithful to the way of Jesus, has characteristically faced society in three ways – in compassion, in confrontation, and in offering a contrast.

Facing the world with compassion

The parable of the Good Samaritan in Luke 10 has been a lasting inspiration to followers of Jesus. It's true that Jesus was not telling the story directly, to say that we should be helping the neighbour who's just been mugged on the way home, but rather was saying that the most unlikely and unsuitable person may be the neighbour who helps us. He turned the question round to answer 'Who is my helpful neighbour?' rather than 'Who should I help?' Nevertheless, the inspiration is clear and the phrase 'being a Good Samaritan' has penetrated our culture, even through to regular use in the tabloid press.

The Church has obeyed that call of compassion with impressive thoroughness. It is estimated that each month churchgoers give 23 million hours of voluntary service outside what they do in their own churches. Over half a million children under 16 are involved in Church of England youth and children's activities in addition to any involvement in church worship. The churches collectively are far and away the largest voluntary organization in the country.

Healthcare has always been a preoccupation of the followers of Jesus, who spent much of his ministry bringing wholeness of body and mind to people who were troubled. The first systems of healthcare were founded by the Church (e.g. the monasteries, and the Knights Hospitallers in Jerusalem providing medical help for pilgrims from about 1080). Eventually these systems developed into hospitals. Florence Nightingale was motivated by her faith to reform the nursing profession after her traumatic experience in the Crimean War. Following the ministry of Jesus, Christian care of lepers in Africa has been legendary, the iconic example being Albert Schweitzer's work in Lambarene. The hospice movement has clear Christian origins in the vision of Dame Cecily Saunders. And today 40 per cent of all primary healthcare in sub-Saharan Africa is delivered by the churches. This has been a remarkable response to the healing example of Jesus.

Education has been a similar preoccupation of the followers of Jesus. By the late sixth century in England, schools were being established in monasteries and cathedrals to enable future monks and priests to be able to read and write and eventually to become learned in Greek and Latin texts suitable to their vocation. Grammar schools, Oxford and Cambridge universities, and a number of now famous schools and colleges were all established by Christian bodies in the Middle Ages, and the commitment to education was sustained through the centuries to the point where most of the schools before the nineteenth century were still being run by the churches. The Ragged Schools Union taught over 300,000 of the poorest children in London through the middle years of the nineteenth century. Now approximately one quarter of primary schools in England and Wales are church schools. The effect of the living Jesus in education has been immense.

The history of voluntary organizations and charities in the West is largely the story of Christian people propelled into action by their faith in the face of some sad distress or unmet social need. Most bishops are bewildered by the number of charities they find they are patrons of, and clergy are forever serving as trustees of local charities and getting involved in any number of good works. Often people don't know about the Christian roots of the big national charities. The Oxford Committee for Famine Relief was first founded in 1942 by Anglicans and Quakers to relieve the suffering of Greeks as a result of the Allied blockade. Today *Oxfam* works with over 3,000 partners in 100 countries.

In 1961 Peter Benenson, a Roman Catholic, was outraged by reports that two Portuguese students had been sentenced to seven years in prison for raising their glasses in a toast to freedom. He wrote an article in *The Observer* newspaper inviting people to write letters in support of the students, and the huge response brought about the founding of *Amnesty International* (AI) at a meeting of seven mainly Christian men in Luxembourg that same year. AI now sets the standard as a campaigning organization for political prisoners.

The Revd Chad Varah founded the *Samaritans* in 1953 'to befriend the suicidal and despairing' after taking the funeral of a 13-year-old girl who had killed herself. There are now 202 branches of the Samaritans in the UK, with 15,500 volunteers, and the international arm, Befrienders Worldwide, operates in 40 countries. Chad Varah continued to serve in Anglican parishes and to champion the needs of the sexually vulnerable.

Development and relief charities such as *Christian Aid*, *CAFOD* and *Tearfund* have obvious Christian origins, and each has a very considerable impact both at home in its campaigning and abroad in partnerships with local churches and other groups. *Traidcraft* was established by Christians in 1979 to fight poverty through fair trade. They innovate, campaign and build lasting relationships with their 100 supplier groups in 30 developing countries, and are regarded as setting benchmarks in fair trade practice.

The *Children's Society* was founded in 1881 by Prebendary Edward Rudolf to reach out to those forgotten children who face danger or disadvantage in their lives, children who are in trouble with the law, young runaways on the street, disabled children and young refugees. All this work is intentionally based on the Christian principles of love, justice and forgiveness, and the relationship with the Church of England remains strong.

A less specific effect of the living Jesus in the arena of compassionate activity is the powerful consequence of what might be called *Christian presence.* US President Barack Obama encountered the effectiveness of this presence when he worked for a group of churches in community organizing in Chicago. It led him to a deep respect for the churches as the location of true local commitment to change, and to his own final step from an agnostic upbringing to a personal faith. Simon Jenkins didn't find personal faith but he did find deep respect when he wrote in *The Guardian* that whenever he visited poor places in the UK 'and wondered to whom the desperate turn in time of need, the finger always points to the Church. Of all the voluntary organizations, those based on religion are the most present and the most committed.'[2]

The same thing happened to Matthew Parris when he revisited the Africa he had known as a child. He said after a recent visit,

> Now a confirmed atheist, I've become convinced of the enormous contribution that Christian evangelism makes in Africa: sharply distinct from the work of secular NGOs, government projects and international aid efforts. These alone will not do. Education and training alone will not do. In Africa Christianity changes people's hearts. It brings a spiritual transformation. The rebirth is real. The change is good.

He went on,

> The Christians were always different. Far from having cowed or confined its converts, their faith appeared to have liberated and relaxed them. There was a liveliness, a curiosity, an engagement with the world – a directness in their dealings with others – that seemed to be missing in traditional African life. They stood tall.[3]

Confronting the structures

If I were a fisherman and constantly found that the area where I went fishing seemed only to have dead fish floating in the water, I might be inclined to go upstream and see what was poisoning the water. It's the same principle with confronting the social, industrial and economic structures that seem to be causing distress to God's people and destruction to God's world. It's not enough to offer compassion; what's needed is fundamental engagement with root causes.

Of course, many of the charities mentioned above also engage with problems in these rigorous ways, within the limits of charity law. But followers of Jesus may well find themselves going into the Temple and taking on powerful economic forces on their home ground, just as Jesus did that momentous weekend in Jerusalem. Jesus knew that soft words and gentle optimism wouldn't shift the massive rockfall that blocked the way to freedom and justice for God's people. He went in with a bulldozer.

Many social reformers have had to do that too. Elizabeth Fry, a Quaker, was appalled by the conditions of women prisoners in Newgate Prison and gradually built up a compelling case for reform. By the 1820s she was an irresistible force, and the 1823 Gaols Act started a process of *prison reform* that continues to this day. The long, hard-fought battle of William Wilberforce and Olaudah Equiano to outlaw the *slave trade*, and eventually slavery itself, is well known. Inspired by his evangelical faith and as a member of the Clapham Sect, Wilberforce signed the first draft of his Bill on the same table on which Holy Communion is celebrated at Holy Trinity Clapham even today. Faith and works need each other.

Lord Shaftesbury was another evangelical who recognized the need to guarantee social justice through Parliamentary reform, and he achieved three *Factory Acts* in the mid-nineteenth century, along with the Coal Mines Act (1842) which prevented the work underground of women or children under 13, and the Lunacy Act (1845). Working also in the field of housing, education and the Young Men's Christian Association (YMCA), Shaftesbury had an enormous impact on social conditions in the Victorian age, but it required diplomacy, persistence, stubbornness and high principle. The opposition of vested interests was always deeply entrenched.

Contemporary parallels in this task of confrontation have led the followers of Jesus to take world poverty very seriously indeed. The *Jubilee 2000* movement to persuade wealthy countries to drop the numbing debts of the poorest developing countries was a mass campaign that came straight out of the heart of the churches and their prophetic tradition: 70,000 peaceful, cheerful campaigners came to Birmingham to create a 9 km ring around the venue being used by the G7 leaders. This was serious protest and it got results. Whether those results are being delivered is another question. The *Make Poverty History* campaign flowed straight out of Jubilee 2000 and in 2005 it focused attention on three goals: trade justice, dropping the debt, and more and better aid. It cannot be right that nearly half the world's population live on less than $2 a day, that 800 million people go to bed hungry, or that a child dies of poverty-related causes every three seconds. What on earth or in heaven does God make of that?

Going back a few years – but not all that many – there were other major injustices causing righteous anger among Christians. Foremost among them was *racism*, both in the American south where Martin Luther King Jr raised his voice and was assassinated for it, and in South Africa, where it was institutionalized by law. A year or two ago I was in the museum in Cape Town which stands as a memorial to District 6, the black area near the city centre that the apartheid system needed to shovel out of existence. It was moving to look at the large-scale map covering the whole ground floor of the museum, and to see where families had written their names on the places on the map where their houses had been before demolition. From there we went out to District 6 itself and to the only building that remained – a church. They couldn't demolish a church, it appeared, but it was the message of that church that finally demolished apartheid. 'There is no longer Jew or Greek, there is no longer slave or free, there is no longer male and female; *for all of you are one in Christ Jesus*' (Gal. 3.28).

The Christian witness of the churches was ultimately decisive, and Archbishop Desmond Tutu was in the thick of the battle, but he said his own journey started when as a child he saw Bishop Trevor Huddleston respectfully remove his hat when he passed Tutu's mother in a hospital corridor. Such behaviour was astonishing to a young black child being brought up in the dark heart of apartheid. This was something altogether different and altogether worthwhile. 'All of you are one in Christ Jesus.' He was hooked.

Meanwhile, in the southern USA a young black pastor was panicking. He had just got out of jail and received a death threat on the phone. 'Nigger, if you aren't out of this town in three days, we're going to blow your brains out, and blow up your house.' He sat in the kitchen and thought of his loyal wife and newborn daughter asleep upstairs.

> I bowed down over that cup of coffee. I prayed a prayer that night. I said, 'Lord, I'm down here trying to do what's right. I think I'm right. I think that the cause we represent is right. But Lord, I must confess that I'm weak now. I'm faltering.'

Martin Luther King went on,

> And it seemed at that moment that I could hear an inner voice saying to me, 'Martin Luther, stand up for righteousness. Stand up for justice. Stand up for truth. And I will be with you, to the end of the world.' I heard the voice of Jesus say still to fight on. He promised never to leave me alone. No never alone. No never alone. He promised never to leave me, never to leave me alone.

Three nights later a bomb exploded on the front porch, filling the house with smoke and broken glass, although no-one was injured. But King was ready now. He wasn't turning back.[4]

This is the quality of steadfast confrontation, in the spirit of Jesus standing before Pilate, that changes the rules of our society. It was the same with the fall of *Communism* as a monolithic ideology enslaving millions. The Church somehow embodied the spirit of freedom that the young people longed for and they crowded into the cathedrals as places of inspiration before taking to the streets to demand the end of tyranny. In one Eastern bloc city, the people got out their keys and held them high, jangling them as symbols of their cry of freedom.

The Church represented the Free Man, Jesus, who stands before the world, daring us to believe.

Offering a contrast

We will need to return to the theme of Jesus confronting the tyrannical structures of our time – and every time – in the next chapter, but for now we need to visit the third stance that the Church of God has characteristically taken up in facing the disfigurements of society – the way of contrast. In trying to be faithful to the way of Jesus, Christians have tried to offer a different model of being and belonging, a way of being 'creatively maladjusted' (Martin Luther King's phrase) to the norms of our confused and distracted society. Dominican theologian Timothy Radcliffe writes:

> There should be something about Christians that puzzles people and makes them wonder what is at the heart of our lives . . . Without our lives being in some way odd, if we just conform, then our words about faith will be vacuous.[5]

The challenge to be odd. (Of course, some of us manage that without really trying.)

It goes back a long way. This is an extract from a letter that turned up from the first century:

> Christians are indistinguishable from other people by nationality, language or customs. They do not inhabit separate cities of their own, or speak in a strange dialect, or follow some outlandish way of life. Unlike some other people, they champion no purely human doctrine. With regard to dress, food and manner of life, they follow the customs of whatever city they happen to be living in, whether it's Greek or foreign. And yet there's something extraordinary about their lives. Any country can be their homeland, but for them their homeland, wherever it may be, is a foreign country. They live in the flesh but they are not governed by the desires of the flesh. They pass their days upon earth, but they are citizens of heaven. Obedient to the laws, they yet live on a level that transcends the law . . . In short, what the soul is in the body, Christians are in the world . . . God has appointed them to this great calling, and it would be wrong for them to decline it.   (From the Epistle to Diognetus, *c.*124 AD)

Christians were known by their difference. It's not clear that this would be the distinguishing mark of today's followers of Jesus.

That, however, is our particular calling – to be distinctive, and attractively so, as we live out the Christian difference.

After the Church achieved respectability at the start of the fourth century when Constantine adopted Christianity as the official religion of the Empire, the difference that following Jesus made could easily be lost, so hundreds of men and some women took to the deserts of North Africa to live a life of asceticism, seeking after God. That experience led in turn to communities of hermits gathering together in the desert, and finally to the founding of stable religious communities in more conventional settings, such as Benedict's Monte Cassino in about 529. These communities then mushroomed all over Europe for the next seven centuries. In every case these religious Orders set out to witness to the uniqueness of the Christian calling. This was usually expressed in the three-fold vows of poverty, chastity and obedience, but the underlying spiritual energy lay in living together for Christ in the midst of a darkened world.

Of course, monasteries too could grow fat and lazy and take on the hue of the surrounding culture, including a complacent Church, and it followed that a new protest was needed in order to keep the Christian contrast alive. The Reformation provided the framework for such a 'protest-ant' statement, with the Counter-Reformation as response. All over Europe the great rock of the Roman Church began to fragment as Anabaptists, Mennonites, Amish, Moravians as well as more mainstream Lutheran, Presbyterian and ultimately Baptist and Methodist churches splintered away to keep the purity of different interpretations of the gospel. The tragedy lay in the disintegration of the one Church that could bear united witness to the reconciliation available to all in Jesus Christ, but the aim was always to maintain the Christian difference, to stand on the gospel of Christ and be completely faithful to him.

In the UK the evangelical revival in the eighteenth century saw the emergence of the Methodist Church in defiance of the easy accommodations of the Church of England. Revival was in the air. A Cornish parson, William Haslam, was preaching one day when he found himself caught up in a wonderful sense of peace and didn't quite know what he was saying. After a while wondering at this phenomenon, a man rose up in the congregation and shouted, 'The parson is converted! The parson is converted! Halleluiah!' and bedlam broke out. A parallel revival took place in the nineteenth century when the Oxford Movement brought new life to the catholic end of the Church of England. At the same time other new beginnings were taking place as, for example, when the Salvation Army was founded by William Booth. Years later an old man was found kneeling at the base of a statue to William Booth. He was saying, over and over again, 'Do it again, Lord. Do it again.' There is a longing in the Christian heart constantly to be renewed, to be different from the tawdry compromises of normal living. It's a story of unaccepted failure.

In the twentieth century some church life is undeniably in decline in the West. The situation is much more complex than many vociferous opinion-formers would have us believe. For example, lower numbers in church on Sunday do not necessarily mean a marked drop in religious affiliation. It may simply mean that there are so many other legitimate calls on weekend time in a more complex commercial, leisure and relational society that even a committed Christian may only be in his or her church one Sunday in four. However, there is a discernible frustration with institutional church among the young, and as a result other forms of Christian association and spiritual journeying are very much in evidence. Church often isn't different enough; it doesn't stand before the world with the marks of Jesus. It appears to be in league with the forces of respectable convention in society, and who wants that?

It's not surprising, therefore, that 5,000 young people go to the ecumenical community at Taizé in France every week throughout the summer. The last time I was there, 77 nationalities were represented. The atmosphere is relaxed, self-regulating; worship is open-textured, gentle; conversations are natural, international, generous, exploratory. For many young people it seems as if at last they've glimpsed what they've been looking for. (That, sadly, is not the way the Church appears to most young people.)

Christians aim to follow Jesus, and therefore they keep trying to stand in counter-cultural contrast to the crass selfishness and addictive consumerism of a world that increasingly plays fast and loose with its abundance. We fail. Nothing new in that, unfortunately. But what matters is that, when we've fallen, we get up again. And what also matters is that we think certain things are worth making a fuss about. There's a story told by the poet and philosopher Charles Péguy of a man who died and went to heaven. When he met the recording angel he was asked, 'Show me your wounds.' He replied, 'Wounds? I haven't got any.' The angel said, 'Did you never think that anything was worth fighting for?'

These, then, are the characteristic ways in which Christians face society as they try to follow Jesus – in compassion, in confrontation, and in offering a contrast. There are, however, the makings of a perfect storm brewing up in the future of our fragile globe. The stakes are getting higher. What is the effect of the living Jesus in the face of such odds? Is Jesus up to it? This is what the next chapter is about.

5

Jesus – the world's hope

————•◦•————

Why is it that so many thoughtful young people wouldn't dream of looking to the Church as a natural home for their dreams? When Bishop John V. Taylor's son decided to give up on the Church he said to his father, after they had been to church together, 'Father, that preacher is saying all the right things, but he isn't saying them *to* anybody. He doesn't know where I am and it would never occur to him to ask.'

Perhaps we should ask a lot more than we do, and the answers we get might be quite painful. The Church might be seen by many younger people to have failed because it isn't asking big enough questions. Or rather, it's asking personal, spiritual, introverted questions without addressing the dominant social and global realities they know they're facing – systemic poverty and injustice, global meltdown through climate change, permanent high-level risk of terrorism, and a culture that seems set on consuming itself to death. If the gospel that seems to come from the churches is a thin, shrinking escape from the big pressures of life (big government, big business, big finance, big media), is it any wonder that intelligent young people will say, 'No thanks'?

I'm indebted in this chapter to Brian McLaren, whose book *Everything Must Change*[1] explores how the life and teaching of Jesus address the most critical global problems we're facing today because of the radical 'framing story' he lived and offered. McLaren's images and detailed analysis make a compelling read as he breaks open the big issues which some parts of the Church contrive to avoid.

The domestic agendas of the churches, worrying about sexuality and censorship and who can be a bishop, seem far removed from the robust faith that Dietrich Bonhoeffer wrote of in the introduction to his book *Ethics*: 'Not in the flight of ideas but only in action is freedom. Make up your mind and come out into the tempest of living.'[2] It's into that tempest of living that Jesus plunged himself. He never ducked a big challenge. He walked straight into Jerusalem to challenge the imperial and religious authorities about whose world this really is. He played his King of Diamonds, proclaiming the treasures of the kingdom of God; Pilate responded with his Ace of Clubs as Jesus was hammered on to a cross; but on the third day God trumped everything with his Ace of Hearts – love was come again.

Is our gospel big enough to take on the powers that lay behind Pilate? The powers today are very strong indeed, and so omnipresent that we easily miss them, mistaking them for benign friends. The dominant narratives of our time persuade us that unlimited growth through unrestricted consumption, and a global security system based on fear and domination, are the inevitable norm in the twenty-first century. And usually that seems to be justified because, by and large, we get by, our material well-being grows slowly, and nobody tries to kidnap us as we go to work. But one chief executive likens our situation to a man going off a very high cliff in an aeroplane without an engine. He feels to be flying free with the wind in his face and the world laid out below him. The problem is that although he feels he's flying, in fact he's in freefall. He just doesn't know it yet because the ground is still far away, but it's only a matter of time. It's a chilling picture, but it's based on the honest assessment that every living system of the earth, every life-support system, is in decline. We're living infinitely in a finite world.

The idol of unrestrained consumption

The one thing a politician cannot say is that we must stop trying to make everything bigger. Our appetite for more and more, faster and faster, seems non-negotiable. Industry depends on it. The financial institutions are built on it. The constant bombardment

of our senses by invitations to spend, the subtle coaxing of the adver-
tisers (which disguises an iron intent), the built-in obsolescence
of manufactured goods, the riotous lending of easy money – all
these things are made to look innocent and obvious. Zygmunt
Bauman, in his book *Globalization: The Human Consequences,*[3]
argues that we can see in Western culture a progression from *the
satisfaction of need* to *the promotion of desire* and now a third stage
of *satisfying our every wish*. This 'completes the liberation of the
pleasure principle, purging and disposing of the last residues of
the "reality principle"'. The brakes are now really off, but in a world
of finite resources and global climate change this so-called progress
is simply suicidal.

One fifth of our rainforests have been cleared since 1960;
they are receding at 1 per cent per year. These are the lungs of the
world, absorbing the carbon dioxide that we over-emit in our
addiction to fossil fuels. I met a Roman Catholic priest a year or
two ago who works in the Amazon rainforest running a radio
station that takes on the multi-national loggers, the ranchers
and the apathetic government, and earns him death threats and
obstacles galore. But he knows the truth of his mission. There are
physical limits to the depletion of our environment, if we are to
survive. Protecting our privileged lifestyles at the expense of poor
countries is simply unacceptable. In the USA the emission of
carbon per person per year is estimated to be 24 metric tonnes.
In Zambia the figure is 0.1 metric tonnes. By 2020 one in three
people globally will suffer from shortage of fresh water. It can't
go on. Addictive consumption in a finite world leads to disaster.

The reality of climate change is the single Big Fact that governments all over the world have to address with absolute seriousness.
The earth is very thin-skinned. Carbon dioxide particles in the
atmosphere rose from 180 to 280 per million in half a million
years, but in the last 150 years they have risen from 280 to 380
(and mainly in the last 50 years). This has been the effect of human
industrialized consumption, leading to level-rises running at 1,000
times the previous or 'normal' rate. There is a saying in Saudi:
'My father rode a camel. I drive a car. My son flies a jet. His son

will ride a camel.' And of course the poor will suffer most. 'Forget about making poverty history,' someone said. 'Climate change will make poverty permanent.'

However, against this alarming backdrop another set of processes is at work. The combination of unrestrained consumption and a rapidly exhausted environment makes responsible behaviour by large corporations essential. But they too are locked into the idolatry of growth-at-all-costs. Brian McLaren makes the point with devastating clarity by writing of a documentary in the USA which attempted to demonstrate what some big business corporations are like (not all, of course).[4] It said the characteristics were:

- showing a callous disregard for the feelings of others, such as when sweat-shop workers are used to produce branded goods for big stores;
- being unable to maintain lasting relationships – so if workers demand a more just wage the firm fires them and moves to another place where it can hire cheaper labour;
- showing reckless disregard for the safety of others, as if health and safety was for another planet;
- habitually lying and conning others when it's in their own interests – spinning the facts;
- failing to conform to social norms in terms of the law, if they can get away with it;
- being incapable of experiencing guilt. Profit justifies anything.

The documentary then explains that these six characteristics come from *The Diagnostic and Statistical Manual of Mental Disorders*, the psychiatric 'bible', and they would together constitute the diagnosis of a psychopath. (Read those characteristics again and you'll see it.) The combination of psychopathic tendencies in business and unrestricted consumer desire in the public creates a lethal mix for the environment. And one of the signs of this is the way that money itself has become decoupled from reality; it doesn't have to attach to anything, such as land, property or gold bars. It has become pure plastic, and the point of the world's financial institutions is to keep it moving. Timothy Radcliffe says, 'So money has become the point of everything, the ultimate goal of human striving, the universal symbol, whose demands are absolute, the final reference point.'[5] Lord Myners was appointed City Minister to clean up the City's financial institutions. In 2009 he announced his intention to resign. He said, 'I am increasingly exercised and concerned with the fact that we have compromised our lives. This is very evident in the financial community – that money has become everything. The absence of clear moral purpose is very troubling.' Lord Myners is going to study theology and ethics. Is theology the only discipline strong or broad enough to tackle the underlying idolatries of our time?

Jesus in the mix

Such a serious situation requires more than a few choice biblical quotes in response. It can only be tackled at the most fundamental level of world-view, the 'framing story' that we live in and believe in. This is where the framing story of Jesus becomes crucial. He spoke constantly of the kingdom of God, the just and gentle rule of God that was breaking in with him, and that offered the framing story that would enable all God's creatures to celebrate their own identity and integrity. He asked people to leave behind the dysfunctional world-view of domination and violence that Rome and the Jerusalem authorities offered, and to opt into the new story of the kingdom, where everyone is treated with dignity and natural limits are respected ('Consider the lilies of the field, how they grow; they neither toil nor spin, yet I tell you even Solomon in all his glory was not clothed like one of these'; Matt. 6.28–29). This is a kingdom of the Common Good, you might say – a kingdom of Love, though that last word must not be seen in sentimental terms but rather as the dynamic energy that creates worlds.

Examine all Jesus' teaching, his parables, his prophetic actions, from this perspective of the kingdom of the Common Good, and you'll find a radical and exciting hope for a new world now, not a fluffy escape to an insubstantial heaven after death. 'Your kingdom come *on earth* . . .' Caesar's world-view of domination is suicidal, said Jesus. Transfer your trust to a new world-view where everyone benefits and everyone knows their limits, and see how everything comes to life (John 10.10). You simply cannot live on more and more bread (Luke 4.4). The addictive behaviour of mega-consumption is a dead end – literally – for both the rich and the poor, because our exhausted planet just cannot sustain it. But there is a glorious alternative, offered by Jesus. The problem was that the entrenched powers living in the old narrative couldn't begin to countenance that new alternative narrative, so they destroyed it (they thought) on Good Friday.

The Church, if it is to follow Jesus, is going to have constantly and boldly to hold out to people and to nations the framing story of the kingdom of God, the kingdom of the Common Good. U2 frontman Bono said, 'Distance does not decide who is your brother and who is not. The Church is going to have to become the conscience of the free market if it's to have any meaning in the world – and stop being its apologist.'[6] Which takes us back to how a lot of thoughtful young people see the Church, and how far we have slipped from the alternative framing story Jesus gave us.

Mind the gap

The consequence of this addictive behaviour by business and consumers in the wealthy countries of the world is that the gap between rich and poor widens. And what happens when the poor look over the fence and see the extravagances of the rich? They get resentful; and when the gap gets wider still, they get angry. The rich put up stronger security fences; armed guards appear; the angry crowd outside becomes a mob – and then someone starts shooting. It's all too predictable and all too common on the world scene.

Inequality in wealth distribution is a colossal scandal. The richest 1 per cent of the world's population owns almost 40 per cent of its total wealth, and the richest 5 per cent owns 70 per cent. The assets of the world's three richest individuals exceed the combined gross domestic product of the world's 48 poorest countries.[7] Would you like to read that last sentence again? In 1969 the incomes of the wealthiest 20 per cent of the world's population were 30 times higher than those of the poorest 20 per cent. But now they are 83 times higher.[8] That's what is meant by the widening gap between rich and poor. It's important, of course, not simply to blame the rich or for us to feel permanent personal guilt. It's not that our wealth causes the poverty of the poor; it's that the systemic injustice of the world's structures contributes to both the wealth of the rich and the poverty of the poor. Nevertheless, those unjust structures need tackling by those best able to do so, and that is inevitably those who have their hands closest to the levers of political, financial and commercial power. Us.

What would God make of the following statistics? If 10 per cent of the world's military budget were spent instead on foreign aid and development, this would care for the basic needs of the entire world's poor. One half of 1 per cent of the US military budget would cut hunger in half in Africa by 2015.[9] As it is, 30,000 children die of hunger and poverty-related disease every day. It's a silent holocaust that has become invisible, so shocking is it to contemplate.

Again, there is little purpose in throwing a few verses at this massive problem of inequality ('You always have the poor with you . . .' Matthew 26.11, or more hopefully, 'Love your neighbour as yourself,' Matthew 19.19). What is needed is a more thoroughgoing realignment at the level of the framing story we inhabit, the narrative we live by and tell to ourselves and our children. And here we encounter the way that Jesus' framing story of the kingdom is fundamentally a story about justice. We are offered by Jesus, with conviction and urgency, the injunction to 'strive first for the kingdom of God and his righteousness' (Matt. 6.33) as our absolutely first priority. Then the other things we need fall in behind it. But keep first things first, he says. The way Jesus puts this it's obvious that the kingdom and God's justice are almost the same thing. You cannot have a world under God's oversight in which inequality on our scale is acceptable.

Jesus told many parables that subverted the system of inequality that we seem to tolerate. For example, a landowner agrees to hire day labourers for a full day's work at a recognized price, and at the end of the day he hires more labourers at just the same price for only the last bit of the day (Matt. 20.1–16). The early-day labourers are scandalized because this is so unfair, but God's justice goes beyond such simple mathematical equality. This isn't inequality; it's sheer generosity, and that's the economy of grace that God offers in his kingdom. Everything is levelled up, not levelled down. In Luke 16 Jesus tells a story about a manager who got into trouble with his landowner for poor handling of his assets. He thought fast and decided to halve the debts of the tenant farmers who owed the landowner money, in order to have friends if he lost his job. The landowner commends the manager, much to the surprise of today's readers. But that only shows how disposed we are to see the story through the eyes of the wealthy. 'This must be unfair,' we complain. However, Jesus sees the whole system as unjust (whereby small farmers get into debt and are bought out cheaply by wealthy landowners). 'By reducing an unfair debt that would further advantage the rich and further oppress the poor, the steward is actually decreasing injustice by assisting the disadvantaged tenant farmers, so he is praised for being shrewd.'[10] He opts out of the dominant system by which the rich get richer and the poor get poorer.

The scandal of global inequality is almost too heinous to imagine. It will probably be seen by future generations as the most enormous blind-spot of the late-modern period. All the time, however, there has been an alternative framing story for us to choose – the kingdom of Relational Justice which, alongside the kingdom of the Common Good, could yet get us through the chicane of disaster which our idolatries of unrestrained growth and unfettered inequality have been setting up for us to crash into. The impact of Jesus' teaching is still on offer. As G. K. Chesterton said, 'The Christian ideal has not been tried and found wanting; it has been found difficult and not tried.'[11]

There's a parable about a very large table covered with a huge tablecloth where great numbers of us are sitting and feasting. The table is groaning with good food. Every seat is taken, except one, saved for the Unseen Guest. Occasionally we're aware there's some movement from under the table; a hand appears, or we hear a cry. There must be a great crowd under there. They have no food; people scramble for anything that falls off our table; sometimes we pass the odd plateful down; sometimes we just push them back under the table. Then suddenly Jesus comes into the room. We expect him to go and take the seat we've left for the Unseen Guest, but no – he lifts up the tablecloth and dives in among the people down there. We're a bit disappointed, even affronted, especially when we hear laughter and singing and freedom songs coming from down there. Then the tablecloth lifts and out comes Jesus with a little child and then a procession of people from under the table, and they form a great circle standing around our table. It's silent; something has to happen. And then someone suggests that if we shorten the table legs radically we can stretch out the cloth that's over the table, so there would be room for us all to sit down together on the cloth and there would be food enough for everyone. 'Shall we do that?' he asks.[12]

That's the question the world keeps ducking.

The idol of aggressive security

Let's go back to that picture of the poor looking over the fence and getting more and more resentful at the unrestrained luxury they see inside the charmed enclave of the rich. As they get angrier, the rich start putting in more security systems with electrified fences and armed guards; the tension increases, until eventually a shot rings out – and the dogs of war are finally released. As the West experiences the growing resentment and resistance of the rest of the world, so it grows more fearful and feels the need to arm itself still more, which in turn of course twists the spiral of mistrust even further. The cycle is tragic and potentially suicidal.

What makes it worse is that the very countries that feel most threatened insist on arming the rest of the world in order to help their balance of payments. The five permanent member countries of the UN Security Council have cornered nearly 87 per cent of the global arms trade.[13] The United Nations says that every day more than 1,000 innocent people are killed by conventional weapons. The story of the millions of landmines biding their time just beneath the surface of our fields, waiting to maim innocent children, is one of the cruellest and most despicable tales of our time. Ex-President Carter once said, 'We cannot have it both ways. We can't be both the world's leading champion of peace and the world's leading supplier of arms.'[14] In recent years the USA, the UK and France have earned more by arms sales to developing countries than they have given those countries in aid. Is this a madhouse? Is there something I've missed?

Martin Luther King laid bare the vacuity and hopelessness of violence more than most. He spoke of the world having a choice: 'either a world at peace or a world in pieces'. He said that 'the chain reaction of evil – hate begetting hate, wars producing more wars – must be broken, or we shall be plunged into the dark abyss of annihilation'.[15] The problem lies in a deadly combination of the spiral of fear and false security hooking on to humankind's addiction to war as something that gives life meaning, taking it beyond the trivia, pettiness and boredom that many people experience in times of peace. This is no criticism of the armed forces themselves, who in my experience in the UK are among the most thoughtful, humane and courageous people I have met. Their loyal service of their country is astonishingly mature and restrained. But they serve a system that's in the grip of a global myth of aggressive security, that believes that the answer to major problems must lie in 'victory' rather than reconciliation, and domination rather than agreement. (In spite of the fact that practically every war ends with people talking to each other.)

It all depends, again, on which 'framing story' we choose to inhabit. Is it the story of 'us' versus 'them', or is it the story of 'us'? The seventeenth-century French bishop and mystic François Fenelon said, 'All wars are civil wars, because all men are brothers. Each one owes infinitely more to the human race than to the particular country in which he was born.'[16] Jesus gave us a vivid, compelling and adventurous alternative to the idol of aggressive security; we might call it the kingdom of Intentional Peace. 'You have heard that it was said, "You shall love your neighbour and hate your enemy." But I say to you, "Love your enemies and pray for those who persecute you"' (Matt. 5.43–44). If anyone thinks that's a soft alternative they ought to try it. Jesus' strategy was one of peace-making ('they shall be called children of God'). It involved turning the other cheek, walking the extra mile, making peace on the way to court – looking always to the relationship rather than to the regulation.

The most vivid demonstration of the alternative world-views on display here is seen on Palm Sunday, when with a little historical imagination you can see two processions arriving in Jerusalem. One was from Caesarea (or Rome). It was for Pilate, the Roman governor, who spent most of his time in Caesarea to be near the cooling sea breeze and the news from Rome. Jerusalem, by contrast, was a place of heat and flies and sweaty crowds and crazy religious fanatics – not a place to spend much time. But you had to put in an appearance at the major festivals to show who was boss, and to remind the tens of thousands of pilgrims who poured into Jerusalem that Rome was mightier than any tin-pot rebellion they might be tempted to start. The symbol of Pilate's procession was his war-horse, thundering in from the west.

On the other side of town, coming in from the east, from Jericho, was a very different procession. It was for this extraordinary young teacher everyone was talking about, and it was a most strange affair. Jesus mounted a dusty young donkey, which probably put him all of 20 centimetres above the crowds around him, and off he went, down the steep hill into the seething city. The disciples knew Jesus was making an important statement, though they weren't quite sure what it was. But they entered into the spirit of the occasion as the locals laid their cloaks on the floor and tore branches off the trees to wave a welcome. That bemused, faithful donkey couldn't have been more different from Pilate's fearsome war-horse.

But then, everything was different. One was a procession of power, the other a procession of peace. One man practised vengeance, the other practised forgiveness. One leader silenced opposition, the other loved his enemies. One would do anything to save his skin (would wash his hands of anything, in fact), the other would do anything to be faithful to his heavenly Father.

So which procession shall we join? And before we claim too much too soon, let's remember that politically and economically it looks to most people in the world as if we are in Pilate's procession already. It requires a determined choice to leave that procession and join Jesus.

The choice

The basic choice Jesus puts to us in the residually Christian West is 'Which framing story do you want to live by?' There are some strong stories already running and we can recognize them by the idols built deep into the stories, particularly the idol of unrestrained consumption and the idol of aggressive security. The only realistic alternative to these addictions is Jesus' substitute story of the kingdom of God. This kingdom can be variously described as the kingdom of the Common Good, the kingdom of Relational Justice, and the kingdom of Intentional Peace – those are all dimensions of the kingdom Jesus came to set before us.

What matters, however, isn't what we call it; what matters is that we choose it. If we don't choose it – and continue to choose it on a daily basis – we can be sure that we will be swept away by the pervasive narratives that the West has determinedly spun and in which we seem trapped. As ever with addiction-recovery programmes, it seems that only deep springs of spiritual energy are strong enough to break the addiction. Jesus offers a clean alternative, and one we need to write on our bathroom mirrors so we see it first thing every day and last thing every night:

'Strive first for the kingdom of God.'[17]

6

Jesus – crazy about the Church

On the last day of his life, Pope John Paul I said to Cardinal Bernardin Gantin, 'It is Jesus Christ alone we must present to the world. Outside of this, we have no reason to exist.'

That is what the Church is for, to speak about Jesus. Or you could say, with Rowan Williams, that the Church is meant to be the place where Jesus is visibly active in the world. It's where we should be able to see what he's up to. If we are to believe the letters of the New Testament, Jesus is in the closest possible relationship to the Church (the head of the body which makes up the Church, Colossians 1.18), but this all-too-human organization must often drive Jesus to distraction. I imagine Jesus protesting, 'How could they?!' 'They're doing *what*?!' 'But I said . . . !'

I once saw a cartoon with the members of a church council sitting round a table. The vicar is summing up. 'So,' he says, 'the vote is as follows: Stephen, Ruth, Tim, Peter and Jenny are *for* the proposal. God and I are against.' The Church has seen much abuse of power. A notice at a Paris hotel tried to be helpful. 'Leave your values at the front desk,' it said. The Church has seen that happen all too often as well. Indeed, there is not much point in cataloguing the failures of the Church; that would be a depressing and all too accurate tale to tell. Rather, let's see why Jesus is crazy about the Church in the good sense, why he loves it so much he's prepared for it to be called his body (1 Cor. 12.12–31), and his bride (Rev. 19.7).

The intimacy of Christ and his Church is a theological first principle. Listen to how Rowan Williams puts it:

The Church is the community of those who have been 'immersed' in Jesus' life, overwhelmed by it. Those who are baptised have disappeared under the surface of Christ's love and reappeared as different people . . . What is the Church? It is simply those who have been immersed in, soaked in, the life of Jesus, and who have been invited to eat with him and pray to the Father with him.[1]

Similarly, this intimacy is emphasized by Paul, who calls on Christians to 'put on the Lord Jesus Christ' (Rom. 13.14) and, by being 'in Christ', to let ourselves be 'a new creation' (2 Cor. 5.17). Peter says to followers of Jesus, 'you are a chosen race, a royal priesthood, a holy nation, God's own people' (1 Pet. 2.9).

This is a high and glorious calling, and might not immediately remind us of our local church. But we should never lose sight of the fact that the clearest effect of the living Jesus on the world was the coming into being of a body of believers who soon came to be known as the Church. And that body of believers now makes up a third of the world's population.

Early days

Did Jesus intend to found the Church? If the question means did Jesus intend us to have the Church of England General Synod and the Church Representation Rules, I'm glad to report that the answer is no. Fortunately Jesus had no eye for detail (except for the hairs on your head, the sparrow that falls to the ground and the widow who put all she could into the collection plate). But Jesus certainly knew that he was leaving behind a community of believers, and it was on their grasp of the significance of his story, and on their determination to inhabit that story for themselves and share it with others, that he utterly depended. He had no other plans. There were no principles of church growth other than to tell the story. There were no strategies for pastoral care other than to see Christ in everyone and serve him there. There were no service books other than the song that Christ had put in their hearts.

Who was there on the first Easter Day to form the basis of that community of believers? There were 11 disciples, shell-shocked and uncertain after the events of that incredible weekend. There was a group of women who had come with Jesus from Galilee and who had stood with enormous courage just a few yards from the cross when the most harrowing event of their lives had taken place. There were the 120 believers who Peter addressed in Jerusalem in the early days after the resurrection when they needed to replace Judas among the apostles (Acts 1.15). Doubtless there were still many young people around in Galilee who might have been chosen by Jesus when he was deciding on his final line-up of friends to go with him, but who had to go back to the fields and the lake instead. And there were hundreds, maybe thousands, of people who had brushed against the young teacher in his Galilean ministry and had only the warmest of memories of that encounter. And that was about it. It wasn't a lot on which to base the entire future of God's project with humanity.

However, this motley assortment of followers of Jesus turned out to be heroes of the first order. (We shouldn't get carried away, however, by the idealized glow of early 'super-Christians', as if it has all been downhill since then. One writer called the early Church, 'One, Holy, Catholic, Apostolic and Scruffy. Sometimes very scruffy. But still glorious.'[2]) By AD 65 the Church had spread throughout modern-day Turkey, into Greece and as far as Rome. The Greek word for church, *ekklesia*, meant 'a gathering of people at the call of a herald'. In the New Testament the word 'church' never meant a building or a denomination because neither yet existed. For the first 200 years the Church had no buildings of its own; gatherings of Christians took place in houses, which probably meant that they were not more than 20 to 30 strong. Paul mentions several 'house churches', including those run by Prisca and Aquila (Rom. 16.3), Nympha (Col. 4.15) and Philemon (Philemon 2). Realizing that the letters to, say, the Corinthians were addressed to this kind of church can have a strange effect on how we read them – 'is *that* what it was like?' Of course today, too, millions of Christians around the world still meet and worship in houses.

Services in the early Church included teaching, prophecy, singing, readings from Scripture (the 'Old Testament') and perhaps
the latest letter from Paul. At the start they seem to have met daily
but they came to settle mainly on the new 'first day of the week',
i.e. Sunday, the day of resurrection, when the Eucharist quickly
became the characteristic ritual. Sunday was a normal working
day for most people so the services would have taken place either
before or after work. Leadership was given by Paul (and probably
by other church planters) to particular gifted individuals and
couples, but theirs was not the understanding of priesthood that
many churches have today; instead they emphasized the priesthood of all Christian believers (1 Pet. 2.5, 9). However, leadership
became increasingly significant as the churches grew and all
sorts of difficult issues cropped up, so elders (*episkopoi*, overseers)
and deacons (*diakonoi*, servants, responsible for the practical,
charitable action of the Church) became essential.

'And day by day the Lord added to their number those who
were being saved' (Acts 2.47).

So what went wrong?

So far so good, it appears. The Church was growing at a meteoric
rate. Terrible persecutions occurred but the Church only seemed to
get stronger. The impact of the living Jesus was unstoppable. The
puzzle to the modern believer is to understand how this unified
Church, founded on the 'rock' of Peter's leadership and the strong
presence of James, the Lord's brother, could have broken up quite
so spectacularly into the fragmented Church we see today. It is of
course the familiar story of human frailty coming up against divine
beauty; we drop the precious heritage we've been given, feel bad
about it, and spend the rest of our time trying to put it together
again (we call it 'the ecumenical movement').

The big split occurred in 1054. The 'Great Schism' was the
result of a complex, fluctuating relationship between the Eastern
(Greek) Church and the Western (Roman) Church. The Eastern
Church ('Orthodox') disagreed in the creed on whether the Spirit

proceeded from the Son as well as the Father, and rejected the 'monarchical' view of church authority represented by the Pope, preferring a 'conciliar' model which served the four Eastern patriarchates well. Just as great a split occurred in the Western Church at the Reformation in the sixteenth century, when Roman authority and practice was again rejected by many in favour of a more egalitarian church structure and a return to more primitive, biblically based understandings of devotional practice and the Eucharist and, above all, the primacy of faith rather than good works as the route to salvation. The result has been that the Protestant tendency to split when things go wrong has fragmented the Western Church into hundreds of smaller, sometimes quite extraordinary, denominations. The following parody gives something of the flavour of the contemporary bewildering scene in inter-church relations:

I was walking across a bridge one day and I saw a man standing on the edge about to jump off. So I ran over and said, 'Stop! Don't do it!'

He said, 'Why shouldn't I?'

I said, 'Well, there's so much to live for.'

He said, 'Like what?'

I said, 'Well, are you religious or atheist?'

He said, 'Religious.'

I said, 'Me too. Are you Christian or Buddhist?'

He said, 'Christian.'

I said, 'Me too. Are you Catholic or Protestant?'

He said, 'Protestant.'

I said, 'Me too. Are you Anglican or Baptist?'

He said, 'Baptist.'

I said, 'Wow! Me too! Are you Baptist Church of God or Baptist Church of the Lord?'

He said, 'Baptist Church of God.'

I said, 'Me too! Are you Original Baptist Church of God, or are you Reformed Baptist Church of God?'

He said, 'Reformed Baptist Church of God!'

I said, 'Me too! Are you Reformed Baptist Church of God,

reformation of 1879, or Reformed Baptist Church of God, reformation of 1915?'

He said, 'Reformed Baptist Church of God, reformation of 1915.'

I said, 'Die, heretic scum,' and pushed him off the bridge.

To have got to this level of division requires a remarkable degree of disobedience to the plea and prayer of Jesus in John 17.21 'that they may all be one . . . so that the world may believe'. Humanity has a propensity to know better than Jesus and to be clear that truth requires separation from others who have gone astray, and this has ensured that the global Church looks tragically fragmented. As a minister said to his neighbour on leaving an ecumenical meeting, 'We're all doing the Lord's work – you in your way and I in his.' The World Christian Database numbers over 9,000 denominations, while the *World Christian Encyclopaedia* comes up with 33,820!

There is, however, another way of looking at the huge range of denominations we now have worldwide. We could see them as representing different reflections of the character of Jesus. The impact of Jesus has been to cause an explosion of human communities dedicated to following him in ways that make sense to them in their context. Given the vast range of cultures, theologies, personality types, world-views, and political and social histories that we encompass, it's not surprising that when you plant a seed called 'gospel' you get a great range of communities called 'church'. And each of them reflects something different about the character of the universal Christ. The following sketches are inevitably somewhat crude, but they might make the point nevertheless.

- *The Roman Catholic Church* could be said to reflect Jesus' care for the apostolic community, nourished by his body and blood. Jesus was committed to his beloved community of disciples and shared his life with them. So too Jesus cares for his Church, feeding them in the community's core action, the Mass.
- *The Protestant churches* could be said to reflect the way Jesus loved us to death, 'even death on a cross'. The power of the

cross is the mainspring of Protestant theology, opening the way to a new resurrection life which puts sin, sickness, even death, in its place.

- *The Anglican Church* could be said to reflect the passionate balance in Jesus' life whereby he drew on different sources of authority (Scripture, tradition and reason is one way of describing them) and humbly but clearly outlined the way to live well in God's kingdom. Anglicans are committed to exploration and inclusivity, as was Jesus.
- *The Orthodox Church* could be said to reflect the glory of God in the person of Jesus, unchanging and undiminished. To go to Orthodox worship is to enter the timelessness of divine beauty. As one Orthodox worshipper put it, 'When you're in heaven, what's your hurry?' When worshipping in Russia on one visit, and seeing the raw devotion of the *babouschka*, I came to appreciate why Communism was bound to fall – the roots of Holy Russia were too deep to be torn up; eventually they would bring down the false edifice built insecurely over them.
- *The Pentecostal and Charismatic churches* could be said to reflect the life-changing vitality of Jesus and the immediacy of his presence. Jesus promised that his Spirit would live on in his people; here he does just that.

And so the reflections of Jesus' character go on. Perhaps *Methodism* particularly reflects Jesus' concern for the poor, and *Baptist churches* reflect his commitment to radical conversion and change of life in his followers. Perhaps *Quakers* reflect Jesus' constant inner communion with his Father, and *Anabaptists* his challenge to a counter-cultural way of living. In all these churches there appears to be a discernible 'centre of gravity' where some quality of Jesus is highlighted in a particularly vivid way. The fuller marks of a true Church as 'One, Holy, Catholic and Apostolic' can be found in the infrastructure of each of these churches, but there is a special *charism* which each brings, drawn from the infinite riches of Christ.

Nevertheless, we may still look to the day when that 'centre of gravity' is simply Christ, not just a particular element of his life and ministry. Sometimes progress is made in that direction when reports of theological consensus are produced. Sometimes it's when churches at local level are engaged in mission together and differences fall away. Sometimes it's when risky symbolic actions are taken and everyone knows the Spirit has nudged the churches to a new place. In 1966 Pope Paul VI and Archbishop Michael Ramsey celebrated an ecumenical liturgy in Rome. They signed a declaration expressing their desire for unity. Then the Pope took the Archbishop off to show him some frescoes, and suddenly he asked him to take off his episcopal ring. Ramsey was puzzled but did so. Then the Pope slipped his own ring on to the Archbishop's finger, the ring he had worn as Archbishop of Milan. The Archbishop was moved to tears and wore the ring for the rest of his life. It was the ring Archbishop Rowan Williams wore when he went to visit Pope John Paul II decades later.[3] Symbolic action can often move things forward more effectively than a whole shelf of reports.

The Jesus meal

Central to the self-identification of any church is how it remains faithful to the direct challenge of Jesus to 'do this in remembrance of me'. Holy Communion, the Eucharist, the Mass, the Lord's Supper – whatever it is called, this is the defining ritual of most churches and most Christians week by week. The philosopher Feuerbach wrote, 'Man is what he eats,' meaning it as a reductionist statement ('that's all a person is'). However, he couldn't have made a more Christian and sacramental statement; we are indeed what we eat, so as we feed spiritually on Christ in Communion we become like him. The effect of Jesus on human lives could not be clearer.

In fact, Jesus left us two great commands at the Last Supper, symbolized by bread and wine on the table and a towel on the floor. If we pick up both of these, then we are being faithful to our Lord. They are themselves intimately related; as bread and wine are distributed each person receives the same share, one piece of bread, one sip of wine. That is how Christians believe it should be in the world; we should all receive justice and a fair share of the world's good things. In the Eucharist the rumour is confirmed and celebrated that the poor are hearing good news, the captives are being released, the blind are recovering their sight, and the oppressed are going free (Luke 4.18).

It's at this service that we come closest to the heart of what it is to be a Christian. We're exposed to both word and sacrament because we receive the life of Christ in the context of hearing his story. Strangely, of course, we gather together around the altar and re-enter the story at the very point when the community disintegrated. We gather as community to remember when the community fell apart. Yet this is the paradox. Where life has been laid down, there life has been restored. And that's the constant experience of Christians. As we give up our lives and the exhausting pursuit of celebrity status in our own little world, we're given them back, renewed and re-made. As we give up the struggle to be a self-made, self-assured and self-sufficient success, needing nothing but our own genius and a large mirror, so we enter the giving-and-receiving community gathered around the wounded young Prince, and are re-shaped in his image.

What happens? Well, who can say? Interpretation is as rich as the diversity of humankind. The Orthodox say the Eucharist is 'life, light and fire'. Pope Pius X said the Eucharist is the shortest and safest way to heaven. Thomas Merton, the Trappist monk and spiritual writer, said that at the Eucharist, 'I feel washed in the light that is eternity and become one who is agelessly reborn.'[4] Whatever the language, it's clear that people can find nothing more rewarding and appropriate to do at all sorts of moments than to re-inhabit those crucial actions of Jesus. And in doing so they find grace to uphold them in the most dire of situations. Timothy Radcliffe recalls being in Rwanda when terrible violence broke out. He and others were due to visit their Dominican sisters working in refugee camps in the north. They had a horrendous journey through lawless bandit country, but then came the worst.

We saw the utter misery of the refugee camps. We visited a prison that was like an abattoir. We went to a hospital filled with children who had lost their limbs through mines. I remember one child who had lost both legs, one arm and an eye. They had no money to buy crutches let alone artificial limbs, and so they had to hop. And I went outside into the bush and I wept. That evening we celebrated the Eucharist in the sitting room of the sisters. The walls were filled with bullet holes from the recent fighting. When the time came to preach a sermon, I had no words for all that I had seen. I had never met such suffering before. Anything that I could say seemed trite, banal. But I did not have to say anything. I was given something to do, a ritual to perform. We re-enacted what Jesus did on the night before he died. We repeated his words, 'This is my body, given for you.' When we utter words of utter anguish, then we remember that on the cross Jesus made them his own. And when we can find no words at all, not even to scream, then we may take his.[5]

Admittedly that is an extreme example, but the principle remains the same: the Eucharist somehow embraces all human experience, across the whole range of pain and celebration, and enables us to handle experiences too large for us to process by normal means. It was the same when men first went to the moon. As they touched down, Buzz Aldrin on Apollo XI asked Houston for a few moments of silence for reflection and thanksgiving. He wrote later,

For me, this meant taking Communion. In the blackout I opened the little plastic packages which contained bread and wine. I poured wine into the chalice my parish had given me. In the one-sixth gravity of the moon, the wine curled slowly and gracefully up the cup. It was interesting to think that the very first liquid ever poured on the moon, and the first food eaten there, were consecrated elements.[6]

As Dom Gregory Dix wrote many years ago, 'Men (*sic*) have found no better thing than this to do for kings at their crowning and for criminals going to the scaffold; for armies in triumph or for a bride and groom in a little country church . . .' – and he goes on to list every conceivable situation when we have indeed 'done this' in remembrance of him.[7] It speaks for us; it speaks to us; it speaks of us. It is the very life of Jesus, given to us. The Eucharist both looks back to the foundational events of the Christian faith, and acts as an appetizer for the royal banquet to come. As the Holy Community gathers together to receive Holy Communion, so they have a foretaste of the Holy Kingdom that God intends for us all.

Jesus and the future Church

On a bad day, when the computer's having a breakdown and I'm not far off, it can seem as if the Church many of us know and love is on its last legs. Many social factors are running in the opposite direction to the Church's health, and at the same time we in the Church seem to have decided to play vacuous ecclesiastical games instead of trusting Jesus and giving our attention to the world. One writer illustrates the danger like this. Say you invite Jesus to share your home. It's huge fun and leads to lots of laughter as well as stimulating conversation and changes in the running of the house. However, after a while you find Jesus poring over adverts for Christian Aid and Oxfam in the daily paper, and then looking around your rather well-appointed home, and you begin to feel just a bit uncomfortable. You want to take him to church, of course, and that goes well. They love his fresh energy and openness. However, they do find some of what he does worryingly relaxed – even casual. He wants to ask questions in the sermon; he doesn't seem very bothered about some of the conventions and rituals we value; he sings too loudly, almost as if he means it. So the churchwardens wonder if he'd like to try another church down the road. At home he continues to be great company, but he does bring some strange friends back to the house. Finally it all comes to a head when he brings back an entire homeless family of asylum seekers and gives them his room while he sleeps on the landing. It's no good. You decide you'll have to put him into a cupboard, for safety. So that's what you do, and you put a cross and two candles outside the cupboard so people will know he's in there – but not dangerous.

The domestication of Jesus is the Church's continual temptation. The impact of Jesus on the Church can be severely restricted and diminished if we find him too radical and to be asking too much. We settle too easily for comfortable, foam-rubber Christianity and a faith where Jesus is more a friendly pet than an untamed tiger. But if we try to tame this divine tiger we'll all be losers. Fortunately the tiger will always reappear in some other part of the jungle.

To change the image, it sometimes seems to me that spiritually we're living in an arid landscape, 'a dry and weary land where there is no water' (Ps. 63.1). Beneath the surface of the land, however, there are many underground rivers running powerfully, offering a network of strong spiritual resources for a new generation of Christians. These new embodiments of 'church' come in many forms, and a lot of them are based on communities living the faith in new ways. Many 'fresh expressions' of church are committed to their neighbourhoods in deep relationships and social action. The Northumbria Community lives out its Celtic values with imagination and flexibility. The Soul Survivor movement lives in the culture of today's young people but offers a radical alternative vision of what it means to live well. Sant'Egidio in Rome is a lay community dedicated to social justice arising out of prayer. And Taizé is a continuing inspiration to the tens of thousands of young people who go there every summer, living and praying simply and witnessing to reconciliation and peace-making. When Archbishop Rowan Williams was in Taizé in 2009 he said,

> A person may have spent many years going to church, reading the Bible, and saying prayers, and yet never quite have seen the Church – the Church which is the New Jerusalem and the Church which is the hope of humanity. Taizé is such a place.[8]

Jesus' plans for the Church are extraordinary. He sees all humanity gathered together in himself. Or that, at least, is how Paul interprets Jesus (Eph. 1.10). It's a tall order, and not for the faint-hearted. But all God's people will surely say, 'Bring it on!'

7

Jesus – partner in prayer

———— ◦•◦ ————

I was in Cape Town waiting for the installation of Archbishop Thabo Makgoba as the new Primate of the Church of South Africa, and sitting in the shade of a public park next to the cathedral. I was clearly recognizable as a priest and an elderly black woman carrying a big black Bible came past. She stopped and asked if she could pray for me. I rarely refuse such an offer. The prayer contained many confident references to being 'covered with the blood of the Lamb', and while this may not have been my usual vocabulary when praying with a stranger, it was what she was doing with the Bible that gave me more cause for alarm. As she prayed she proceeded to hit me on the head with her Bible and then all the way down to my feet – and back up to my head again. It was her way of 'covering' me, I suppose. I was beginning to feel slightly dizzy and was about to try some cheap British escape like 'I think I'm fully prayed for now, thank you,' when the prayer came to a glorious, final 'Amen'. This isn't quite what I have in mind for this chapter on the effect Jesus has on our praying!

I was thinking more along the lines of how we relate to Jesus in prayer, how central Jesus is to Christian prayer, what we do when we lose touch with Jesus, and so on. When I first became a follower of Jesus in a meaningful sense at university, I can remember one of the most exciting changes was from praying to a distant deity who was little more than a vague philosophical shadow to praying and talking joyfully with a living companion. Walking back to my digs down the Abingdon Road in Oxford became much more exciting and, if I didn't concentrate on the traffic, quite a bit more dangerous. There is a natural intimacy in such prayer.

We read that 'the LORD used to speak to Moses . . . as one speaks to a friend' (Exod. 33.11). Evening dress was not required.

Jesus became essential to Christian prayer as believers realized they were either praying directly to him, or praying to the Father but 'through' Jesus. If they were praying directly to Jesus it was nothing short of astonishing; you don't do that kind of thing to your friends. Here was the man who they had known in all his flesh and blood reality, and now he was well on his way to becoming the second person of the Trinity. If they were praying 'through' Jesus it was as if Jesus was the companion who brought them and their prayers into the halls of heaven and got them a hearing. They prayed 'through Jesus Christ our Lord' because Jesus was the 'router' (in IT terms) through whom prayers went to the Father, or the 'filter' who sifted out the dross in our prayer so that only prayer that had the character and blessing of Jesus came before God. But because of that filter-effect Jesus could say, 'if in my name you ask me for anything, I will do it' (John 14.14). When our prayer has been purified by Jesus, nothing can stop it.

Of course, it doesn't matter if we find ourselves naturally praying to God the Father or to Jesus the Son, or even to the Holy Spirit. It's really a matter of spiritual instinct. But Christian prayer will always have Jesus in the mix. He's the One who carries the prayer to the heart of God.

How Jesus prayed

Of course, the first impact of Jesus on how his followers might pray comes from watching and listening to Jesus himself. His chroniclers noted how 'in the morning, while it was still very dark, he got up and went out to a deserted place, and there he prayed' (Mark 1.35). Christians have been doing something like that ever since. At the start of the day and in a quiet place they have prayed. Some have gone far into deserts for a lifetime to pray; some have laboured long in silence; some have made regular retreats into quiet space; but most serious Christians have found some particular place to pray and very many have found the morning to be the best time.

It's noticeable also that, when Jesus had a particularly momentous decision to make, he fortified himself with a special time of
prayer. When he had to prepare himself for the huge task he knew
he'd been given he went on a long retreat to the wilderness. It
was 40 days and nights of hard work, arguing with himself and
with his devils (Matt. 4.1–11). When he had to choose the 12 who
would travel the dangerous road with him he went off to pray
through the list of possible candidates (Luke 6.12). When he had
to face the Final Question of his life he went to Gethsemane
to have a proper, honest struggle with himself and with his
Father (Mark 14.32–42). As his followers, Christians have done
the same – we have devoted special time to pray before our big
decisions, whether as individuals or as a church. We need to be
full of God if we're to be full of wisdom.

The Gospels are littered with ideas about prayer that can be
learned from the words and practice of Jesus. We learn about the
importance of persistence when he tells the story of the man who
wakes up his friend in the early hours so he can make a sandwich
for a visitor (Luke 11.5–8). We learn about the value of spontaneity
when Jesus suddenly gives thanks that it's the little people who
are catching on (Matt. 11.25–30). We learn about faith when time
after time he hands over somebody in need of healing to the
generosity of his Father's love. (Do we really believe that something
is actually happening when we pray?)

The effect of Jesus on our praying is most clearly seen, however, in the prayer he himself gave us when asked for guidance on
prayer by his friends, a prayer which we have treasured ever since.
Thousands of pilgrims have stood in the Pater Noster Church on
the Mount of Olives and contemplated the endless reciting of
those special words in every language under the sun. Usually when
I'm there we all say the prayer together in whatever different
languages we can muster, the gentle cacophony complemented
perhaps by someone silently signing it as for deaf people. It's very
special to see the prayer written there in Jesus' Aramaic, or to hear
the man in the Coptic chapel above the Church of the Holy
Sepulchre actually saying it in that language. It's the prayer that's

prayed millions of times a day, and it needs to be said slowly. Sometimes I ask a group to stop at one phrase (e.g. 'your will be done') and meditate on it and what it really means, before moving on to the rest of the prayer. Even though I have just said what we're about to do, some people in the group nearly always carry on through the phrase, so used have we become to saying it 'parrot fashion'. We need to let the prayer breathe, to give it space to fill our hearts. Each phrase weighs a ton.

So how do we make this journey of prayer with Jesus our companion? What are the likely milestones on the way? How good and bad does it get? How does the spiritual life change? Let's look at the journey.

Love at first sight

It seems increasingly to me that at the heart of our spiritual pilgrimage is something fundamentally to do with seeing, with seeing deeply. Jesus says to John's disciples, 'Come and see'; Philip said to Nathanael, 'Come and see' (both in John 1). Jesus said to Nicodemus: 'No-one can *see* the kingdom of God without being born from above.' The healing of a blind man in John 9 is an extended exploration of what it means to gain our 'sight', and it's the 'blind' guides who stop people properly 'seeing'. And so on through the Gospels, especially in John.

Sight may therefore be a helpful metaphor for our spiritual journey and the effect of the living Jesus on our prayer. We start with love at *first sight*, or perhaps more accurately, the *sight* we experience with *first love*. The fact is that sight and interpretation are closely linked. We don't automatically recognize the significance of what we're seeing. Some years ago there was a fad of 'Magic Eye' pictures, where you looked at a visual jumble on a page and were challenged to see the stag in the heather that everyone else had seen ten minutes ago. It often takes us a while to interpret what we are seeing. But when the penny drops it becomes a wonderful moment of disclosure. When one of our daughters was two we showed her a picture on the front of the *Radio Times* – a full-page picture of a pig. 'What's that?' we asked, in the helpful way parents do. There was incomprehension on our daughter's face – then recognition. 'Grandma!' she said. We hid the *Radio Times* after that. But the truth is that at first we often don't interpret correctly what we see. We've 'seen but not seen'.

So in our relationships. When I lived and worked in Durham it was deeply associated for me with my parents. They met on their first day as undergraduates at Durham when, not untypically, my father got the only taxi available in Durham station. A porter rushed up and asked if he could kindly share the taxi with this young lady who was also going to the university. They introduced themselves but thought no more about it, although they met several times in the small world that was the university in those days. But then there came the moment when my father stood at the bottom of Dun Cow Lane just between the cathedral and the theology department and looked up and saw my mother standing at the top of the lane. And then he knew this was the girl he must marry (for which I am very grateful). But that was the moment of 'sight' – first sight, deep sight, interpreted sight – the sight we get with love.

Many of us have such a moment or a period on our spiritual journey when it all comes together like that, and what we've 'seen but not seen' comes into focus. The penny drops and, just as in our human relationships, we love going back over that story, to return to the moment of spiritual first love, to relish it, retell it and be strengthened by it. For many of us who call ourselves Christians this first love is associated with Jesus. He becomes central to our lives and we commit ourselves to following his way of living.

This 'first sight' then, these early experiences of Jesus or of God-in-Christ, are crucial, but what matters about them is that these experiences can feed and shape our Christian growth, or they can feed and shape our spiritual pathologies. They can excite our spiritual passion in ways that inspire a lifetime in the garden of God's delight, or they can imprison us in a small room with bare walls. We all know people who have made a 100 per cent surrender to a 10 per cent idea of Christ. So we need to value the first sight we've had of God's love but not try to tame the great wind that blows where it wills. It's a relationship, and relationships that are not allowed to change ultimately do great damage to the participants. So we need to make sure that our first love, our first sight of Jesus, feeds us with freedom, not the stale air of the prison cell. Scripture mustn't be a dead lump; the sacrament mustn't be a magic brew. We all value our received traditions but those traditions must stay alive. As John Habgood once wrote, 'Tradition is the living faith of the dead, but traditionalism is the dead faith of the living.'

In my own case, however, I was deeply excited by encountering a new Jesus, one I simply hadn't been introduced to before. My Jesus had been two-dimensional and rather tame; now he was vibrant with life, passionate and committed. Lord Hailsham made a similar discovery at one point in his life and he described it like this:

I looked at the Gospel again, and quite suddenly a new portrait seemed to stare at me out of the pages. I had never previously thought of a laughing, joking Jesus, physically strong and active, fond of good company and a glass of wine, telling funny stories, using, as every good teacher does, paradox and exaggeration . . . applying nicknames to his friends, and holding his companions spellbound with his talk . . . As I reflected on this I came to the conclusion that we should have been absolutely entranced by his company.[1]

This was the Jesus I first caught sight of at the age of 19. It wasn't quite love at first sight but it was certainly the first sight of Love.

Second sight

This experience of first sight usually gives way to what we might call simply, *second sight*, a time of maturing, when we start to glimpse the richness of this Christ figure and begin exploring as many of the storehouses of spiritual wisdom as beckon to us. It's when we start finding language, ideas and methods of prayer that feed us and shape us for the long haul. It's when we begin to get a glimpse of the scope of this enterprise of holiness, when we see that it's not painting by numbers but a whole rearrangement of our lives in every department; it's when we begin to see that we're on the edge of an immense ocean, not just king of the paddling pool. It's exciting, and it's essential if our faith is not to shrivel in the heat of life.

If we think of first sight as akin to first love, this move on to second sight is as Pelagia's father says to his daughter in *Captain Corelli's Mandolin*,

> Love is a temporary madness, it erupts like volcanoes and then subsides. And when it subsides you have to make a decision. You have to work out whether your roots have so entwined together that it is inconceivable that you should ever part. Because that is what love is. Love is not breathlessness, it is not excitement, it is not the promulgation of promises of eternal passion . . . That is just being 'in love', which any fool can do. Love itself is what is left over when being in love has burned away.[2]

Gaining second sight is what we do when we decide to pick up our rucksack from the hallowed ground and move on. This is growing up. It's when we begin to gain a deeper understanding of the blistering reality of God's love, when we start to 'comprehend, with all the saints, what is the breadth and length and height and depth, and to know the love of Christ that surpasses knowledge, so that [we] may be filled with all the fullness of God' (Eph. 3.18, 19).

'Second sight' involves, for one thing, educating the spirit and allowing Jesus to broaden our horizons. We embark on serious Bible study, we encounter Taizé or Iona worship, we go on a course on prayer or do a Myers-Briggs workshop, we make a first retreat, we read a book on Ignatian spirituality, we go to a conference on 'Business and the Benedictine Way', we talk to someone about painting and prayer, we discover icons – and so on. The result is that windows fly open; new ideas are in the air and it's very exhilarating, but it can also be very confusing. Christ is a much more complex figure than we'd thought; what do we make of him now? How do we follow and how do we pray? When I was a diocesan youth officer I was in perpetual motion, restlessly pursuing the six new ideas I had each day before breakfast, and giving no time for my soul to catch up. Then at a conference of youth officers a monk said to us, 'Unless you spend half an hour a day in silence, you'll burn up.' That single remark hit me between the eyes; to this day I can see where he stood and where I sat. He was absolutely right, and I've had a love affair with silence ever since. However, he was also telling us not to remain adolescent in our faith. Move on, he was saying – grow.

Developing 'second sight' will take us deeper into the things of God, but it will also engage us with the deeper structures of society around us and the huge social and political implications of the gospel of the kingdom which we were exploring in Chapters 4 and 5. We can no longer be social innocents about issues of justice. We begin to realize that religion and politics are woven on the same loom because justice and human flourishing are funda-mental to any serious faith. God's family knows no boundaries and his kingdom has no borders. Nevertheless, this is sometimes a serious challenge to a narrower, purely 'spiritual' interpretation of faith. To be told that my vote is a spiritual issue is a step some followers of Jesus find hard to take.

There's yet another area of growth to which we are called as we move into this 'second sight'. We start learning more of the riches of Christ, more about the deep structures that make human societies work, *and more also* about the deep structures of our own make-up, what makes us who we are, and how we function. What awaits us here may be an honesty we'd rather not face.

But deep down I do want to understand more of myself and my complex responses, my defences against Jesus and his truth, and my ingrained self-deceptions, because I recognize the truth of what Paul says in Romans 7 that 'I do not understand my own actions. For I do not do what I want, but I do the very thing I hate' (v. 15). So maybe in my spiritual journey I'll start reading Jung and finding a spiritual director, and going on an Enneagram workshop. I might start to relate my personality and my spirituality more creatively and realize that it's OK to be drawn more to some forms of prayer and spiritual journeying than others. That can be quite liberating – I don't need to feel guilty that I can't pray like others do, that I don't need to look pale and slightly pained or float a few inches off the ground, because my own journey has its own authenticity. The riches of Christ are vast enough for each of us to have our own bag full of them.

So our experience of developing *second sight* is full of good things – a growing education of the spirit in different ways of prayer, a growing awareness of the deep structures of the world, leading to more social and political engagement, and a deeper understanding of ourselves and what makes us tick, and how that relates to prayer. First sight, first love; second sight, going deeper. But we have to be honest – at some time or other we're going to need something even more taxing.

Night sight

What we are probably going to need is *night sight*. In other words, at some point on the way, we're going to lose the plot. Jesus has disappeared. The memory of the vitality and freshness of faith that we once had are now a mockery. We feel like the psalmist in Psalm 69:

> I sink in deep mire,
> where there is no foothold;
> I have come into deep waters,
> and the flood sweeps over me.
> I am weary with my crying;
> my throat is parched.
> My eyes grow dim
> with waiting for my God.
>
> (vv. 2–3)

You may know some words that the famous Dutch Roman Catholic writer Henri Nouwen put on paper near the end of his life:

So what about my life of prayer? Do I like to pray? Do I want to pray? Do I spend time praying? Frankly, the answer is no to all three questions. After sixty-three years of life and thirty-eight years of priesthood, my prayer seems as dead as a rock . . . I have paid much attention to prayer, reading about it, writing about it, visiting monasteries, and guiding many people on their spiritual journeys. By now I should be full of spiritual fire, consumed by prayer. Many people think I am and speak to me as if prayer is my greatest gift and deepest desire.

The truth is that I do not feel much, if anything, when I pray. There are no warm emotions, bodily sensations, or mental visions. None of my five senses is being touched – no special smells, no special sounds, no special sights, no special tastes, and no special movements. Whereas for a long time the Spirit acted so clearly through my flesh, now I feel nothing. I have lived with the expectation that prayer would become easier as I grow older and closer to death. But the opposite seems to be happening. The words 'darkness' and 'dryness' seem best to describe my prayer today . . .

Are the darkness and dryness of my prayer signs of God's absence, or are they signs of a presence deeper and wider than my senses can contain? Is the death of my prayer the end of my intimacy with God or the beginning of a new communion, beyond words, emotions, and bodily sensations?[3]

Unfortunately, we'll never know the answer to that, because Henri Nouwen died soon after writing that moving passage. It appears that Mother Teresa experienced something similar for a large part of her life. She wrote, 'I am told God loves me, and yet the reality of darkness and coldness and emptiness is so great that nothing touches my soul. Did I make a mistake in surrendering blindly?'[4] So what are we to say when what we really need is *night sight*, a way to see in the dark, when there's a grey dust over everything that once sparkled and shone? When Jesus has gone absent without leave?

The first thing to realize is that we may simply have driven our truck into the sand. We've been on the spiritual road for a long time and we've fallen asleep at the wheel. What we need is someone to haul us out – the spiritual AA. And when we've been hauled out, then we might go back to a safe place, a known landmark, a familiar way of praying and start again, gently. Or we might take it as an invitation to travel on to new places, new oases of the spirit, new ways of praying. I've done both in my time, and been thankful.

Another possibility when everything has gone dead is that we've somehow got our theology askew. Maybe we're looking for God as if he were far away, so transcendent he's almost disappeared. Maybe we think we have to go on a long and perilous journey to find him because he's so *totaliter aliter*, so completely other. But maybe we've got it wrong. Because if the Incarnation means anything it means we have a God who's always seeking us out, not hiding in distant places, a God who's always coming towards us at the speed of light, who presents himself to us so constantly we've almost screened him out. Isn't grace simply God coming to us all the time, in love? And isn't faith simply catching that grace as it flies towards us and appropriating it for ourselves? The problem then isn't the absence of God; it's the absence of *me*! When God calls, I'm often not at home. Indeed, the spiritual writer Martin Laird says simply, 'God doesn't know how to be absent.'[5] What we are dealing with is the illusion of separation from God.

Another way of seeing this is that we may be placing God in a category called 'spectacular'. We may think God can only be experienced in some special way – a warm glow, an amazing event, a healing, the moon turned to blood. And because this isn't the stuff of a wet Wednesday in Walsall, we think God isn't around. But if God really is God, the author and sustainer of every particle of existence, then he's bound to be more around in the ordinary stuff of life, because by definition there are more 'ordinary' than 'extraordinary' things going on. So then it's not a matter of seeking God in the bizarre, but recognizing him in the day-to-day, recognizing the divine watermark that lies in everything.

Of course, there's a third option. Not that we've run into the sand, and not that our theology has become somewhat skewed. It could be that we are being drawn into the apophatic way, the way of silence and waiting and darkness; the end of words and images and feelings. Prayer is then simply hunkering down in the darkness, not trying, not searching, but waiting, longing for a drop of moisture on a parched tongue. Yet God is closer to us than we are to ourselves. We may not sense the presence of Jesus, but his Spirit breathes silently within us, we in him and he in us.

Whichever of these is our experience, it's then that we need *night sight*, and much patience. But God is in it just as surely as he was in that first sight, our first love. His beautiful but terrifying love doesn't change – we just have to realize it's a wilder, riskier experience than we thought we'd signed up for. We need to hang on. And hopefully, as our eyes get used to the dark, we'll recognize the familiar outline of Jesus, waiting for us.

In-sight

Night sight will often lead on to another part of our journey with Jesus. First sight, second sight, night sight – now *in-sight*. When Peter came back from his nightmare of denying his Lord, he was asked three times by Jesus whether he loved him. 'Yes, Lord. You know that I love you,' said Peter, again three times (John 21.15–17). He did love him, but at a deeper, more realistic level than before. He had been on a huge journey, and he had come back a wiser, more humble and more modest disciple. So do we. When we've been through dark places we don't come back with the same bright-eyed innocence we had before. Our eyes have been opened. It's tough out there following Jesus when he passes through Gethsemane and then gets flung on to a cross. So it's a quieter faith we come back with – more modest, more disciplined, with more *in-sight*.

One of the key characteristics of our subsequent life in Christ is the discipline and joy of seeing God as ever-present in the heart of ordinary things. Hopefully we might be seeing the ordinary experiences of life transformed by the presence of a graceful God. We might be wanting to value the common things around us, as did Brother Lawrence, the seventeenth-century French monk who looked after the kitchens and found God as much in his place of work as when he went to chapel. He urged us to 'practise the presence of God'. He wrote:

Love does everything and it's not necessary to have great things to do. I turn my omelette in the pan for the love of God. When it is finished, if I have nothing to do, I prostrate myself on the ground and worship my God, who gave me this grace to make the omelette, after which I arise happier than a king. When I can do nothing else, it is enough to have picked up a straw for the love of God.[6]

The idea is that we do everything for the love of God and in the name of Jesus, as Paul directs in Colossians: 'Whatever you do, in word or deed, do everything in the name of the Lord Jesus, giving thanks to God the Father through him' (Col. 3.17).

In-sight, deep seeing, will also involve relishing the everyday – what's called the sacrament of the present moment. On those occasions when I manage it, I find great benefit in simply slowing up as I walk down the street or through the garden. When we do that we get in touch with our bodies, the feel of the ground under our feet, the rhythm of walking. We get in touch with our environment; we notice the smell of the newly cut grass, we hear the sound of the birds, we see the texture of the tree bark, we notice the sun streaking through the trees, illuminating a cameo of creation. It's transforming. If we go slowly, we find that 'earth's crammed with heaven, and every common bush afire with God,' as Elizabeth Barrett Browning has it.[7] Ordinary things may suddenly pulsate with life. A poppy I once found, which had turned its glorious face towards me as I looked out of my window, simply swallowed me up. On Easter morning a few years ago in Canterbury Cathedral, I was in procession down the main aisle, the sun was pouring in, the organ thundered, there was music and joy everywhere, and my daughter turned towards me with her wonderful smile. I couldn't sing another note. The sacrament of the present moment.

In-sight is when God transforms the everyday into something deeper and more resonant. George Herbert was used to finding 'heaven in ordinary'. In one of his poems, now a favourite hymn, he wrote,

> Teach me, my God and king,
> In all things thee to see;
> And what I do in anything
> To do it as for thee.

A man that looks on glass,
On it may stay his eye;
Or, if he pleaseth, through it pass,
And then the heaven espy.

This is the experience of *in-sight*, when we're probably more at ease with ourselves and with God, more accepting of others, more able to use a wide-angle lens.

And underneath these insights we may become conscious of a new longing, a yearning for a deeper union with Christ. We begin to realize that it isn't sufficient just to follow Christ; more, we are called to *become like* Christ. John Stott, the grand old man of English evangelicalism, in his last public address at the Keswick Convention in 2007, said:

> I remember very vividly that the question that perplexed me as a younger Christian was this: what is God's purpose for his people? Granted that we have been converted, granted that we have been saved and received new life in Jesus Christ, what comes next? . . . I want to share with you where my mind has come to rest, as I approach the end of my pilgrimage on earth, and it is: *God wants his people to become like Christ. Christlikeness is the will of God for the people of God.*[8]

Perhaps the most important 'in-sight' on our journey is that God's purpose is not that we should be religious at all, not caught up in defining true doctrine and deciding who's in and who's out of God's favour; rather, we should simply focus on Jesus Christ and on becoming as much like him as time and grace allow. 'I want to know Christ and the power of his resurrection . . . *by becoming like him* . . .' (Phil. 3.10). And occasionally it's our privilege to meet someone who's well on the way. God's task in us is nothing short of a comprehensive transformation. It's a slow job. As I look at my own life, I find I can echo the words of the ex-slave trader John Newton: 'I am not what I ought to be; I am not what I wish to be; I am not what I hope to be; but, by the grace of God, I am not what I was.'

Out of sight

And then – may we talk of it? – we may find ourselves almost *out of sight*. Not because we are in any way better than others, or more advanced in our knowledge of Christ, but simply because we find ourselves talking about vision rather than sight. Sight seems too flat a concept, too mundane. The vision of God seems a more appropriate language. The glorious, all-embracing vision that silences even the bravest soul. Almost. Because George Herbert, in one of his most extraordinary and brilliant poems, reaches out to the farthest reaches of language and attempts a collection of words and images too rich to take in with one hearing. But here they are: in his poem called simply 'Prayer'.

> Prayer the Church's banquet, Angels' age,
> God's breath in man returning to his birth,
> The soul in paraphrase, heart in pilgrimage,
> The Christian plummet sounding heaven and earth.
>
> Engine against the Almighty, sinner's tower,
> Reversed thunder, Christ-side-piercing spear,
> The six-days world transposing in an hour,
> A kind of tune, which all things hear and fear;
>
> Softness, and peace, and joy, and love, and bliss,
> Exalted Manna, gladness of the best,
> Heaven in ordinary, man well dressed,
> The Milky Way, the bird of Paradise,
>
> Church-bells beyond the stars heard, the soul's blood,
> The land of spices; something understood.[9]

No, I don't understand it either, but somehow, I suspect, it's all there. First sight, second sight, night-sight, in-sight, and finally 'out of sight' – the vision of God.

'For it is the God who said "Let light shine out of darkness", who has shone in our hearts, to give the light of the knowledge of the glory of God in the face of Jesus Christ' (2 Cor. 4.6).

8

Jesus – in a world of pain

After the Boxing Day tsunami of 2005 I remember watching a news report on television which showed a man who had lost his wife and five children, as well as home and livelihood. I was pierced. How do you survive mentally and emotionally after that? Archibald Tait, Dean of Carlisle and later Archbishop of Canterbury, in March 1856 lost five of his daughters to scarlet fever. That silent nursery must have asked terrible questions of his faith.

When one of our daughters was on a gap year in Uganda and working at a school in the hills with many orphans, little Patrick wrote about the best day of his life and the worst day. The best was in Kampala. 'I found a European man in the Sheraton hotel and he asked that do you like football and I answered him that I liked so much. Within two minutes he gave me a football. That's my best day of my life now.' And the worst? 'It was when my father was died and my mother became a mad woman. I was five years old when he died.'

Tragedy is universal and often determines the direction of a person's life. Elie Wiesel was 16 when he was sent to Auschwitz.

Never shall I forget that night, the first night in camp, which has turned my life into one long night, seven times cursed and seven times sealed. Never shall I forget that smoke. Never shall I forget the little faces of the children whose bodies I saw turned into wreaths of smoke beneath a silent blue sky. Never shall I forget those flames which consumed my faith forever. Never shall I forget those moments which murdered my God and my soul and turned my dreams to dust. Never shall I forget these things, even if I am condemned to live as long as God himself. Never.[1]

The accusations mount with every person's experience of life. We all bring something to the table. So where is Jesus in a world so familiar with pain? It's one of the sharpest tests of the relevance and impact of Jesus. Has he made any difference?

Jesus as compassionate presence

If you are a follower of Jesus you watch him closely to see how he handles hard situations. When he is confronted by people in pain you note that he doesn't simply throw out healings like a mad magician; the impression we gain is that he engages the person and finds out more about him or her. He listens. 'What do you want me to do for you?' he says to the blind beggar near Jericho (Luke 18.41). 'Do you want to be made well?' he asks the somewhat surprised paralysed man at the Pool of Bethesda (John 5.6). 'Has no one condemned you?' he asks the woman caught at the wrong moment with her lover (John 8.10). Jesus wants to know more about what it's like to be this particular person in this particular situation. He doesn't want to deal in platitudes or cheap deals.

The first gift of Jesus to a world of pain is endless compassion. We don't have an abstract 'impassible' Deity – that is, one who can feel no pain. We have a Man of Sorrows, acquainted with grief, who cried at the news of the death of his friend Lazarus (John 11.35). Compassion means 'to suffer with' someone. When we attend to another person, and truly give ourselves to the bewilderment and chaos another person is experiencing, some of that person's grief transfers to us. We do more than share it – we inhale it, absorb it, and that can be destabilizing. When we are listening to someone else's pain we need to have one foot in the river with the drowning person and the other on the bank to keep us from being swept away.

The first thing a person in pain wants is someone to listen. And the best listening is done with very few words but with complete attention to the other. How rare that gift is! So often we do our listening to people with an angle, an agenda, a personal need, even if it's only demonstrating to ourselves and to others that we are selfless and skilful. To give ourselves to another is exhausting. I have in my mind the image of Jesus struggling to enter the chaotic world of the woman he met by a well in Samaria (John 4). He stays with her, trying to see what she really wants and needs, trying to get to the heart of her restless serial relationships. This is precisely what the skilled therapist in the counselling room and the willing friend at the kitchen table both offer – a readiness to travel with the person in pain, the incomparable gift of a listening presence.

When I had a nervous collapse after a huge, successful but particularly stressful youth event as a diocesan youth officer, I knew the person I needed to see was a Christian doctor with whom I had been doing some work for the Mothers' Union. Whenever I went to see her she gave me just what I needed – an accepting presence, a few decisive actions ('lie down, sleep') and just enough interpretation of my state to make it tolerable. Above all she was a safe place. The compassion of Jesus has enabled countless followers to offer themselves as a safe place for others.

Jesus as bearer of pain

Sometimes, carefully, with a person suffering deeply, it can be helpful to point beyond his or her personal agony to the cross of Jesus, not in order to deny the pain but in order to give it a shared location. At the cross Christians believe we are looking at the pain at the heart of God. This is not a God of remote distance, coolly appraising his ravaged garden. This is a God of close and intimate involvement who knows 'the hopes and fears of all the years', including what happens to love in a dangerous world. Love gets crucified. If we dare to love we are bound to experience pain; they are two sides of the same coin. C. S. Lewis wrote:

To love at all is to be vulnerable. Love anything, and your heart will certainly be wrung and possibly be broken. If you want to make sure of keeping it intact, you must give your heart to no-one, not even to an animal. Wrap it carefully round with hobbies and little luxuries; avoid all entanglements; lock it up safe in the casket or coffin of your selfishness. But in that casket – safe, dark, motionless, airless – it will change. It will not be broken; it will become unbreakable, impenetrable, irredeemable. The alternative to tragedy, or at least to the risk of tragedy, is damnation. The only place outside Heaven where you can be perfectly safe from all the dangers and perturbations of love is Hell.[2]

The end of the line for the vulnerable love of which Lewis writes is to be crucified. Perfect love attracts the perfect storm. Jesus had lived out the dream in the heart of God, a life perfectly attuned to the Father, one never out of tune with the divine melody. But that was too much for a broken, out-of-tune world; such harmony had to be destroyed and the chosen method was the cross. The result was both more terrible and more glorious than anyone could have imagined, but a part of that result is that we have a picture of permanent value to those who suffer, and a symbol of lasting power about the nature of God. The cross is a devastating image, representing the unthinkable – the crucified God. In a radio broadcast Richard Coles told of the death of his friend Hugo with AIDS. Richard had some experience of church but it had seemed irrelevant. However, on the night Hugo was dying in hospital Richard called to mind the images of Christ that he remembered and tried to find some comfort in them:

I went through Christ the Light of the world, but there was no light; Christ the King, but there was no kingly glory that I could see; Christ the Comforter, but I felt no sense of comfort; Christ the Healer . . . I thought of Christ the first-century social worker . . . promising to make everything better when nothing could make anything better, proclaiming that everything was all right when nothing was. I went out of the room for a cigarette and watched Hugo on the monitor set up in the ward. It was then that I saw another image of Christ before me – Christ crucified – Christ nailed on the cross, scourged, bleeding, ruined. And it wasn't difficult to make the connection. What did seeing the crucified Christ in Hugo mean? What was in evidence that night [was] a dying man's suffering, his wit and strength, a group of friends around him, a gentle exchange, a taking leave. And it was in these things that Christ was truly revealed; through them came comfort and confidence and calm. Not a cheap, fingers crossed, wish against wish, but the grace of God; grace in the arms of catastrophe, unmistakable and overflowing. Hugo died the next afternoon.[3]

It is the awesome grace of the cross to change the unspeakable into something bearable. Many a priest has pressed a small cross into the hands of someone in extremis. The cross speaks; there is comfort, presence, understanding. The cross is both a vulnerable symbol of life's fragility and also a majestic symbol that towers over the human landscape. Lives move in different directions at the cross. Some find the deepest reflection of God's love, others experience the death of belief. As we have seen, Elie Wiesel found it to be the place where his God was murdered. In the foreword to one edition of Wiesel's book *Night*, the French novelist François Mauriac tells of Wiesel coming to see him soon after the war. One of the dreadful experiences Wiesel had seen was the hanging of a child. Mauriac wrote:

I, who believe that God is love, what answer could I give my young questioner, whose dark eyes still held the reflection of that angelic sadness which had appeared one day upon the face of the hanged child? . . . Did I affirm that the stumbling block to his faith was the cornerstone of mine, and that the conformity between the Cross and the suffering of human beings was in my eyes the key to that impenetrable mystery whereon the faith of his childhood had perished? This is what I should have told this Jewish child. But I could only embrace him, weeping.[4]

Not the time, then, for Mauriac to point to the cross, except to do so in his own stillness. But the cross was nevertheless the only way for him to make any sense of perhaps the greatest crime of human history. 'The conformity between the Cross and the suffering of human beings' has been the discovery of countless people in the hardest places. Other faiths have their key concepts and images; Christianity has a symbol of huge power to embody its realism about the dark side of life. What's more, that symbol captures the most crucial battle of all – that between love and all that would destroy love (which we call evil). And we find that love, though defeated, is invincible.

In *Harry Potter and the Philosopher's Stone* Quirrel, working for the evil Voldemort, is strangely impotent when he tries to kill Harry. Harry asks Dumbledore why Quirrel couldn't touch him and Dumbledore replies:

> Your mother died to save you. If there is one thing Voldemort cannot understand, it's love. Love as powerful as your mother's love for you leaves its own mark. Not a visible sign [but] to have been loved so deeply, even though the person who loved us is gone, will give us protection for ever . . . It was agony for Quirrel, full of hatred, greed and ambition, to touch a person marked by something so good.[5]

Jesus was marked by 'something so good', the love of his Father that was his constant confidence. 'You are my Son, the Beloved; with you I am well pleased,' is what Jesus heard at his baptism (Mark 1.11), and he lived in that love all his life. So although at the cross Jesus was sucked into the darkness and the darkness broke him, it also broke itself. The figure on the cross might be configured differently, not as a crippled figure but as an athlete, poised, ready for the resurrection life where Love alone holds the field.

Jesus as source of understanding

Followers of Jesus may share his compassion and, in the right circumstances, point people to the powerful vulnerability of the cross, but there may also come a time and place when we can explore together why bad things happen to good people and what sense all this suffering can possibly make in a world that believers claim is God's. Much faith has been shipwrecked on the rocky shore of suffering. Indeed, the very viability of belief in God is severely tested by the ubiquity of tragedy. In Kate Atkinson's novel *When Will There Be Good News?* there is the following passage:

> Mrs MacDonald had 'got' religion (goodness knows where from) shortly after her tumour was diagnosed. These two things were not unrelated. Reggie thought that if she was being eaten alive by cancer she might start believing in God because it would be nice to think that someone out there cared, although Mrs MacDonald's God didn't really seem the caring sort, in fact quite the opposite, indifferent to human suffering and intent on reckless destruction.[6]

It's the sheer bloodiness of life that brings many sensitive people to non-belief in the Christian understanding of God. They say that if God is all-loving and all-powerful these terrible things would not happen. But they do. So either he isn't all-loving or he isn't all-powerful. Which is it to be? Indeed, they conclude that he isn't either, since such an agonizing world is compelling evidence that he doesn't exist.

The Christian approaches this deeply serious charge by asking what picture of God it is that the atheist doesn't believe in. If God were the Cosmic Plumber who could 'fix' things if he chose to and for some inscrutable reason chooses not to, or if he were a Celestial Puppeteer who could control people's actions but instead lets them kill each other, then indeed we would have an insurmountable problem. But that is not the God that Jesus speaks of. Jesus speaks of the Divine Lover, whose love is so reckless it will go to the cross rather than compromise. This is a God who ties one arm behind his back rather than overwhelm our integrity by forcing his will upon us. He values our freedom supremely because love is the essence of our humanity, and true love can only exist between free beings. It's worth paying the price for that kind of love – the price being the freedom which may lead to accident which in turn may lead to suffering. Rowan Williams says of the cross, 'This is what the price of unrestricted love looks like.'[7]

Freedom for humans means freedom for all creation. You can't have one without the other since the fabric of creation is a unity, and so we have the melancholy list of the charge sheet of suffering. Faced with this possibility of random suffering, should God have 'pressed the button' on creation in the first place? It's Dostoevsky's question in *The Brothers Karamazov*: if God can't create without the suffering of even one innocent creature, then why bother at all? 'I merely most respectfully return the ticket,' says Alyosha's brother.[8] But if there is no other conceivable environment in which autonomous human agents could have evolved so that they could love and be courageous and compassionate and creative and forgiving and so on, then the stark choice is between this world or nothing. That's the ultimate choice for us all. It's a high-risk strategy. The question is – was it worth it?

Jesus is the ultimate example of the freedom God gives his creation. Here is the utterly Free Man – who pays the price of freedom with his life. In a world where the price tags are all mixed up, true freedom looks to be going against the grain, to be subversive and dangerous. But the freedom embodied in Jesus has inspired others to claim their freedom too. Near Riga in Latvia in 1863 some Christians wanted to protest against restrictions on worship and started to plant large crosses on the hill nearby. George Carey writes,

> During the Second World War the Hill of Crosses became a sign of defiance of Nazi occupation, and after the war it continued as a silent protest against Russian oppression. Time after time German and Russian invaders bulldozed the crosses, but overnight they would spring up again. It was an amazing sight: thousands and thousands of crosses, large and small, plain and ornate, all shades of colour, crowded the small hill.[9]

Here we see the cross of Jesus as a symbol of freedom. There was no clearer way of demonstrating the persistence of freedom in the

hearts of the occupied people of Latvia than to re-present, constantly, the Free Man who understood the link between freedom
and suffering because he took them both into himself and died
at the scene of the accident.

We live in the aftermath of the events of Good Friday and
Easter Day but we share the benefits for ever. A few years ago
British people were horrified by an entirely unprovoked attack
on a young mother called Abigail Witchell who was walking with
her 21-month-old son in a country lane near her home in Surrey.
She happened to be a Christian, like her mother Sheila Hollins,
who was President of the Royal College of Psychiatrists, and who
wrote of her daughter,

> The miracle of Abigail's life is enough of a miracle for me . . .
> The attack left her paralysed, and on the night of her injury,
> doctors questioned the wisdom of ventilating her, and then
> had difficulty finding an intensive-care bed for her. On
> that night and in the seven weeks that followed, it was her
> survival, and the life of her unborn child, that we prayed for.
> During these first weeks Abigail started writing poetry, each
> letter slowly blinked out to her patient father. This haiku
> shows how she encouraged us:
>
> > Still silent body
> > But within my spirit sings
> > Dancing in love-light
>
> It is not that Abigail is a saint, but that God's goodness
> has shown itself through the outpouring of love for her by
> the thousands who have been so affected by her story. Per-
> haps the love and prayers are not dependent on anything
> Abigail does or does not do; rather that she has simply been
> a channel of God's peace.[10]

This is just one example of the strange fruit of suffering where
somehow, in the shadow of Jesus' suffering, people manage to
make music with what remains. It doesn't automatically justify
God creating a universe so costly and so raw – the question

still has to be answered by each one of us for ourselves – but it demonstrates how the living Jesus continues to work his way through human lives.

Jesus – reversing the flow

Resurrection is the characteristic activity of Jesus in the lives of his people. It reverses the flow of pain, despair and negativity which is so often the narrative in which we live. It may come like the sun gradually creeping across a landscape, or it may come like a burst of divine energy in a life bound in lethargy, but it comes as we open ourselves to the love behind the story of Easter. In a world of pain Jesus inhabits the compassionate presence of his followers alongside his fellow sufferers; on the cross he embodies the God who bears pain alongside his people; and in the cross-resurrection he placards for all time the risk and cost of love, paid that we should be free. Christians have found that the last word lies with resurrection, the redeeming of what seemed to be 'love's labours lost'. Nothing is ultimately lost with a God who raises the dead.

Tied in as we are to a dying culture obsessed with growth, success, glamour and acquisition, and yet faced with perennially disturbing questions by evil, suffering and mortality, the reality of resurrection flowing from the life of Jesus is completely counter-intuitive. Dennis Lennon writes, 'To be a Christian means to be always young, in a sense more profound than mere biological youthfulness. In the risen Christ the Christian is always at the beginning of life.'[11]

The impact of the presence of Jesus in a world of pain is the possibility of resurrection.

9

Jesus – in the mind of the artist

————•◦•————

The American poet Emily Dickinson once wrote: 'Tell all the truth, but tell it slant.'[1] Some of the most provocative and stimulating explorations of the significance of Jesus have come from the oblique direction of the creative arts. Christianity has been 'telling it slant' for nearly 2,000 years in music and painting, in literature and poetry, in drama and architecture. In churches down the ages there have been wall paintings, stained glass, the sacred theatre of the Eucharist, the biblical drama itself, symbols, light, darkness, music. All telling it slant. Because 'the Word became flesh' God has been embodied in human life, and artists have embodied the Word ever since, in all sorts of ways. The danger is that parts of the Church would have us revert to the word again, or a lot of words. And that would be tragic because it's evident that our minds are much more like art galleries than libraries – we flourish on images much more than on concepts.

The arts are as near as many people are prepared to go towards what we somewhat loosely call 'spirituality'. For some the arts are an end in themselves, an alternative to spiritual practice or religious belief. For others the arts are the threshold of an awakening, a window into the divine; they might choose to go further, they might indeed climb through the window. Or they might just study the window frame and the glass. Either way, the arts can be a safe place to explore all kinds of issues, from beauty and wonder to forgiveness and love, from evil and violence to loneliness and guilt. And time and again, the arts come back to the figure of Jesus.

When he was Director of the National Gallery, Neil MacGregor said:

Luther would have argued that the reason you have to focus on the word rather than the image is because the word is certain and clear and univalent, and the image is necessarily ambiguous and therefore cannot confidently lead you to truth. Well, not many of us now think that language can do that either; it's a notion of language that's completely unsustainable . . . The extraordinary thing about [works of art] is that they offer you a completely other way of organising the world and asking the questions. I think people are very quickly aware of that, and very quickly enriched.[2]

Does that ring bells? Do the arts enable people to find another way of organizing the world and asking the questions? I hope so.

I believe that the arts do indeed help people to engage with deep questions, and they do it in a way more aligned to 'right-brain' thinking – more holistic, intuitive, imaginative. It's the age of the image, of allusion, of telling it slant. In any case, anything that smacks too much of 'institutional religion' brings all the defensive artillery on to the front lawn, but the arts provide common ground. In simple terms, the arts connect. They connect people with something profound and perhaps unsettling, something demanding exploration, taking us deep. In particular, they take us beyond the tyranny of rationality.

Ah, but that's the problem, the secularist would say. Why on earth do you want to go beyond rationality? Richard Dawkins said in a debate,

The B minor mass and the Matthew Passion happen to be on a religious theme, but they might as well not be. They're beautiful music on a great poetic theme, but we could still go on enjoying them without believing in any of that supernatural rubbish.[3]

When asked on *Desert Island Discs* how an atheist could enjoy religious music he said, 'You might as well say how can you enjoy *Wuthering Heights* when you know that Cathy and Heathcliff never really existed. It's fiction. It's good fiction. It's moving fiction. But it's still fiction.'

But only, I suggest, if you're already imprisoned by the tyranny of rationality. Rationality is wonderful – as far as it goes. Some of us find God in the deep rationality of the universe and the fact that rational minds can respond to such intelligibility. But the arts are more playful; they tell the truth, but they tell it differently; they go beyond rationality, and convey truths otherwise unavailable to the human search.

The arts – doorway, or alternative, to faith?

So what is it precisely that the arts do? In spiritual terms, are the arts a doorway to faith, or an alternative to faith? Of course, they can be both, but either way it seems to be true that an increasing number of people, including young people, explore their spirituality through the arts. It connects.

Take music. Inspired by the birth, life and particularly the Passion of Jesus, musicians have produced some of the most sublime music known to humankind. Passions, requiems and masses have poured from their pens, sponsored by the Church and by private patrons who wanted the highest art to echo the highest of themes. I know one cathedral dean who started his journey to faith through hearing the St John Passion and being overwhelmed by it. When I was Archdeacon of Canterbury, on the evening of Good Friday when the great church was exhausted with the emotion of the day, the choir would sing one of the great requiems – Fauré, Duruflé and others – because there was nothing one could say or do that was more evocative and complete. The music said it all.

Music can often speak a language of blessing to people more richly than priestly assurances. The great cellist Pablo Casals said,

For the past 80 years I've started each day in the same way. It's not a mechanical routine but something essential to my daily life. I go to the piano and play two preludes and fugues by Bach. I can't think of doing otherwise. It's a sort of benediction on the house. But that's not its only meaning for me. It's a rediscovery of the world of which I have the joy of being a part. It fills me with an awareness of the wonder of life, with a feeling of the incredible marvel of being a human being.[4]

Music for Casals was a stairway to heaven but also a route to human freedom. It affirmed his humanity. Flaubert, in *Madame Bovary*, said, 'We long to make music that will melt the stars'[5] and that describes the longing that music evokes, the reaching out, the hunger for more meaning, for music that will flood and save the world. At a funeral the choice of music is often the most serious and significant decision that has to be made. I went to a funeral in which a piece by Tavener made the most exquisite statement about finitude and hope. Words could not have done it.

Hymns too carry vast amounts of emotional freight. There are more arguments about the choice, range, tempo, volume, length, taste, cost, ownership and acceptability of hymns and songs than probably anything else in church life. However, the life and death of Jesus has been the springboard for an outpouring of music, the like of which no other life has even touched. Charles Wesley alone wrote 5,500 hymns, most of which took Jesus as their inspiration and focus. Hymns carry our theology. They take the weight at weddings, funerals and great occasions, from the Cup Final to the Coronation. They express our joy, our sense of magnitude and fullness. In bereavement they bring out our tears. They speak of the creative strength of God and the persuasive subtlety of the Spirit, but they most often come home to the life of God Incarnate. 'How sweet the name of Jesus sounds' to so many hymn writers. They might ask, 'And did those feet in ancient times walk upon England's mountains green?' (answer: no), or they might write of the 'amazing grace . . . that saved a wretch like me'; they might want to 'crown him with many crowns' or to see him as 'the Servant King who calls us now to follow him'; they might transport us to the 'Sabbath rest by Galilee . . . where Jesus knelt to share with thee the silence of eternity' or simply marvel at 'what a friend we have in Jesus', but however they write about him, Jesus is the irresistible magnet who has drawn the finest hymns out of the most devoted musicians. And, quite simply, music changes lives.

To a believer, the sadness is people stopping outside the door of the Great Musician, unable to believe that a Musician lives there. People can only be invited to suspend their disbelief and try the door.

Painting – reverence and questioning

So, I believe, the arts are a highway to transcendence. I've only written so far about music, but when you go into an art gallery you see people standing before paintings in silent, almost religious, reverence. In the Millennium year 2000 the National Gallery staged an exhibition called 'Seeing Salvation' which surprised the Gallery by its huge success. I can remember standing before Zurbaran's painting of *The Bound Lamb* and being absolutely transfixed. It struck me dumb as a metaphor for the bound Christ. At the Caravaggio exhibition a year or two later the two paintings of *The Supper at Emmaus*, done at quite different periods of his life and telling such different stories, were spellbinding. I often explore the resurrection with groups, basing it on those two paintings – one resurrection full of light, colour and hope, the other resurrection full of the pain and ambiguity of the cross and the puzzle of the future.

Great painting has this arresting effect on people. It even unnerves the atheist. George Melly, the jazz performer and avowed atheist, was an art collector, and he once made this confession:

> Let me say something – I feel awe, and very like religious awe, in front of certain paintings – by Piero della Francesca particularly. These are paintings of great radiance and simplicity done by a believer – and I cannot but be awed in front of them, especially the one in which Christ is baptised. It does slightly throw me that I am so impressed by pictures painted with a specific religious reason, and to express a faith.[6]

That's the power of art.

As with music, Jesus has been the inspiration of great painting, from the icons of the early centuries to the medieval and Renaissance art sponsored by the Church, and then to the eighteenth- and nineteenth-century paintings trying to express the romance of Jesus' life. Even now contemporary art is often haunted by the symbolic iconography of Christianity, most particularly the ambiguity of the cross, as we see in Stanley Spencer, Georges Rouault, Marc Chagall or Salvador Dali. In the world of painting, you can't really get away from Jesus.

Film – the new theological milieu

In the United Kingdom 3.5 million people go to the movies every week, and often the religious issues embedded in the films are positively legion. One professor of philosophy said this about the film *The Matrix* some years ago:

> The film reinvents religion, updating the messiah myth. It may have the effect of making religion seem cool. Neo is the handsome and charismatic Christ-figure, diffident at first, but maturing into his divinity, who blasts the evil ones, known as the Agents, eventually gaining control over the Matrix. This is the New Testament story for people raised on video games, Star Wars and extreme fighting. Jesus Christ with cool shades and a beltful of guns. I'm not saying this is a good way to recast the central characters of Christianity, but it's hard to deny its cultural impact . . . The fact is that movies are the most powerful cultural influence we have today.[7]

There is, however, a seemingly impenetrable problem with portraying Jesus. He's impossible to pin down. (What would you expect with such a multi-dimensional figure?) In the early days of film the answer was simply to avoid direct portrayal – a voice, or at most a back view, would suffice. I still remember the shock of seeing Pasolini's Marxist Jesus, black and white, powerful, intense, uncompromising, striding from one sharp encounter with the authorities to another. The film was called *The Gospel According to St Matthew* and its origin lay in Pasolini being trapped in a hotel room where, bored, he picked up a copy of the New Testament from the bedside table and read through Matthew's Gospel. He was so startled by what he found there he decided to make a film using as text only the words of the Gospel itself. The film overturns the tables of those who want a fluffy Jesus as a comfortable friend. He hurries through the Palestinian hills, meeting friend and foe with a steady gaze and an awkward question, and you're left thinking he may not have lasted long in an Anglican theological college.

Other films have depicted Jesus with a similar mix of authenticity and fantasy. *Jesus of Montreal* is a humane, contemporary parable, but fails at the resurrection. *Godspell* usefully employs the clown metaphor but stretches it past breaking point. *Jesus Christ Superstar* scores well on high-energy music but fails (because it doesn't even try) to grasp the divinity-in-the-humanity. More recently Mel Gibson's bloody film *The Passion of the Christ* spares us nothing of the agony but fails to give us any glimpse of why so many people would soon give their lives for him. It does, however, in the last 90 seconds of the film, offer the most convincing, tentative interpretation of the resurrection I have yet seen on film.

These films are building on a deeper tradition of theatrical portrayals of Jesus, portrayals that were much less coy in their handling of the key figure. The medieval Mystery Plays were robust and honest, often humorous, and wonderfully literalistic. The Passion Play at Oberammergau is a remarkable survivor and still manages to be profoundly moving for hundreds of thousands of people every ten years. Out of this rich theatrical humus film-makers have been much more cautious and confused, but there is no denying the theological potential of film as one of the great story-tellers and cultural myth-makers of today.

Films can also be remarkably prescient about the future. They are often exploring big themes and coming dangers before most of us are even thinking about them. There were planes plunging into buildings, tsunamis wiping out communities, and climate change causing catastrophic sea rises, as well as reality TV shows, towering infernos and biological warfare, some time before they became real in our experience. We need to stay in touch with this medium if we're to enter the world of young people, and see how they see a world that might be theirs.

The return of story-telling (did it ever go away?)

Story-telling itself is an art form that has been making a comeback in recent years. There are many more professional or semi-professional story-tellers around today, taking us back to our innate fascination with story. So when the story of Jesus is put into the hands of a good story-teller the effect can be astonishing. I have seen one-person performances of the whole of Mark's Gospel and the even longer John's Gospel and been transfixed. All over the country there are people using an approach called Godly Play to tell the Bible stories in a way that captivates young minds and starts them wondering, often eliciting the most thoughtful and unusual responses. The television series *The Storykeepers* was a runaway success, telling biblical stories for children through a clever methodology. The story of Jesus holds its ancient power; we just need to trust the story and tell it.

Truth is so often carried in story form. Harvey Cox wrote:

> We know that we are something more than mere hairless bipeds because of our parables, jokes, sagas, fairy tales, myths, fables, epics and stories. Not only have we created innumerable stories, we have also found endless ways to recount them. We dance them, draw them, mime them with masks and carve them on rocks. We sing them around tables stacked with the cold remains of a dinner. We whisper them in the ears of sleepy children in darkened bedrooms. We stammer them out to confessors and therapists. We inscribe them in letters and diaries. As soon as our young can comprehend our words we begin to tell them stories, and the hope we harbour for our elders is that we will be able to hear their full story before they go.[8]

Story-telling is a tremendously powerful medium. I once led a group where we started each session by asking everyone to tell us something about their past week. The disclosures, the depth, the bonding of that group, telling their own recent stories, was astonishing. We may not have all the arguments, but we all have our own stories, and the telling of those stories is the most powerful and persuasive way of sharing the faith that energizes us.

Worship and more

Worship is an art form in itself and a supreme way of responding to the story of Jesus. We can touch deep places by the imaginative use of Scripture and story, of light and darkness, of music and visuals, of poetry and unexpected readings. The drama of the Eucharist is the great crucible where *daily* life and *eternal* life are kneaded together and worked into our own lives. Liturgy (worship) is in many ways the highest form of art because it's where the Divine Artist encounters his creation and gently and playfully restores it to its natural beauty.

I often end a weekend away with a Christian group with a do-it-yourself Communion service. We spend the first hour or so in groups poring over readings and poetry books to select material to fit into different points of the service. Some will be doing their own creative writing to offer in the worship – poetry, reflections, letters to God. Another group will be choosing music to play or sing, choosing from as wide a range as they like. Another group will be working on prayers – looking in books, writing their own, devising symbolic actions. Yet another group will be working on the visual presentation of the altar, taking material from the woods outside or the materials I've brought for them to use, including clay, nails, silver foil and so on. Sometimes they make me a stole to wear in the service. Another group may be making bread and a wine substitute. I go round seeing what is emerging, and moulding and shaping the material into a liturgy. It truly becomes 'the work of the people' – the core meaning of the word 'liturgy'.

The use of the arts sometimes comes together in special places. Visiting special holy places can have a profound effect on young people. When I was a residentiary canon of Canterbury Cathedral I used to see it again and again. The young people were silent; they would wander off by themselves; you would see them looking up (how rarely we look up these days!). They would look thoughtful – they might just have been thinking of getting to Starbucks or how to chat up a particular girl, but I think there was often much more going on.

The aesthetic experience of churches often combines with some profound human experience to evoke that shimmering moment of disclosure – the awareness of Presence. We may not be able to articulate that experience with any precision, but I'm fascinated by the number of people I interview for ordination who have had some teenage encounter with the numinous, often in a special place, and who later recognized and owned that experience as a major step on their journey.

There was an account in a Sunday newspaper by a woman journalist who had had a baby when she had been told she couldn't. She said,

> As I write this, my son is 21 months old, weighs 14 kilos and has nearly all his teeth. He laughs and runs around in circles. He is sunny and happy and when he was small the French called him *sage* – a high compliment meaning quiet and content. Every mother thinks their child is extraordinary, but I know my baby is more – he is a miracle. Because of the treatment I got in New York, I believe in science and medicine. I believe in not taking no for an answer. But I also believe in something else, something higher. When Luca was tiny, and I was still nervous about taking him outside, our first excursion outside was to a beautiful church, St Roch, near our home in Paris. The church was dimly lit by candles and smelt of old wax and lemons. A choir was practising for Sunday Mass. I sat with my little boy and cried and cried. Later, I asked a friend who is very wise why that

happened. 'I just felt overcome by emotion,' I said. 'It was the strangest thing.' My friend was quiet for a moment. 'It's because you see your son as a miracle,' he said gently. 'And at St Roch you were in the presence of whoever granted you that miracle.'[9]

Churches are often crucibles of aesthetic material – music, architecture, beauty, history, prayer, a sense of place, the centring story of Jesus. The results can be powerful. In that writer's case she experienced release and presence, but many other things happen to people in churches. They gather up many of the elements of aesthetics that this chapter has been about, and while they don't *subvert* rationality, they certainly go *beyond* it.

Censorship and the arts

I love the story of George Bernard Shaw, the playwright, sending a note to Winston Churchill saying: 'I am enclosing two tickets for the first night of my new play. Bring a friend – if you have one.' Churchill replied: 'Cannot possibly attend first night, will attend second – if there is one.'

Not all art is worth a second night. Some is mediocre, some is in poor taste. In the latter case, when a play, a piece of art, a book or a film is downright offensive to believers, is there a case for censorship? My own view is that censorship is nearly always self-defeating. In the first place it discloses a defensive attitude to a rather sad, small image of God. God is God, not a vulnerable elderly relative. If the God of the universe, who 'laid the foundation of the earth . . . who determined its measurements . . . who stretched the line upon it . . . who laid its cornerstone when the morning stars sang together' (Job 38.4–7), if this God is threatened by an ill-judged play in a passing moment in a far corner of his universe, then we have some serious theological reconstruction to do. To think we need to defend God is dishonouring to the majesty of the God of all creation. In any case, how often do you see Jesus standing on his dignity?

In the second place, Christians who plead for censorship are on very slippery ground. When freedom of expression is lost, all sorts of demons file in through the back door. The burning of books has always been seen as a desperate authoritarian act and the prelude to great oppression. Christians are utterly committed to, welded to, the truth. If we pursue the truth we bump into Jesus, because he is 'the way, the truth and the life'. When we hide behind defensive legislation we are distrusting the truth, not believing that truth has to triumph because it's aligned to the nature of reality. Censorship means we are all losers.

Telling it slant

The history of the arts in the West is to a considerable extent the history of the Christian faith. The story of Jesus and the transcendent reality that he embodied has inspired artists of faith and of no faith to explore the meaning of the most significant figure in history. The arts allow people to come at the Christian story in an oblique manner, not having to pay at the door but rather being able to skirmish with Jesus and to explore the liminal spaces that he himself so enjoyed. The arts are a great leveller. We all approach with a full purse, equal in our hunger and appreciation. In music, painting, drama, poetry, film, sculpture and more, we find the finest artists of our day and every day, responding to the life, death and new life of the man of whom it was said, 'in him all the fullness of God was pleased to dwell' (Col. 1.19).

You can't get a bigger subject for your artistic endeavour than that.

10

Jesus – in a world of faiths

There was a television series called *Around the World in Eighty Faiths* which did what it said. The whimsical presenter took us on a whistle-stop tour of 80 of the world's faiths, with special emphasis on the more bizarre expressions of religion. For example, you could wonder why snake-handling had been elevated to such high status for some Christians in Kentucky, or why a mud ceremony seemed necessary for another spiritual encounter. There was plenty of material by which the non-believer could be both reinforced in his or her scepticism, and also disturbed by the extraordinary prevalence of faith. And for the Christian the question posed was: 'Where does Jesus fit into all this?'

Every year in Oxford there is a Faiths Walk when several hundred members of the city's diverse faith communities walk through the crowded streets from a synagogue via a church to a mosque, in order to witness to the friendship which exists between the faith groups in the city. It's a stirring occasion, much helped by the generous helpings of Eastern cuisine freely offered at the end of the walk. Banners are held aloft, balloons wave in the wind, conversation and smiles are all around. But 'true believers' of any of the faiths may well be asking if it is all a compromise. I am sure it is not, but nevertheless the other question is always present – what lies beyond friendship?

Of course, it's often a considerable achievement to have got as far as friendship. The starting position for people of different faiths has often been no higher than *tolerance*. We try to get along without contact and without being rude. The step beyond tolerance, however, is *encounter*. When I was newly ordained in

Birmingham, 'People to People Week' took us into each other's holy places and the effect on a young curate was as strange as it was liberating. So this is what motivated and gave meaning to my Hindu friend who ran the corner shop in Balsall Heath. And this is what energized my two young Buddhist colleagues in the struggle for world development. Beyond tolerance and encounter lies *empathy*. This is where mere touristic interest graduates into an imaginative standing alongside my neighbour of another faith, and this in turn may hopefully lead into genuine enjoyment of the other person in *friendship*. As Archbishop Rowan Williams said when he visited St Philip's Interfaith Centre in Leicester, the issue is not so much one of interfaith relations as human relations. This is not 'my Muslim friend' but 'my friend'.

And yet the question remains: what lies beyond friendship? If I make such grandiose claims for Jesus as I have done in this book, what happens when the hard questions of truth, uniqueness and salvation start to be asked?

Jesus viewed from other faiths

Jesus is a global figure and other faith traditions have had to reflect on his significance. The results are interesting. Muslims, for example, have great respect for Jesus. The Qur'an has a number of references to Jesus and they are not derogatory. Geoffrey Parrinder wrote that 'the Qur'an gives a greater number of honourable titles to Jesus than to any other figure of the past'.[1] Muslims add, 'May God bless him' whenever they mention the name of Jesus. He is called 'a sign', a 'mercy', a 'witness', an 'example'. There is significant respect for Jesus in Islam.

Many Hindus also revere Jesus. Writing in the early nineteenth century, Raja Ram Mohan Roy wrote of the moral teaching of Jesus, 'I found the doctrine of Christ more conducive to inculcate moral principles and better adapted to rational beings than any other that has come to my knowledge.'[2] Mahatma Gandhi could be wittily acerbic about Christians. 'I love your Christ,' he once said, 'but I hate your Christians; they are so unlike him.' But he could only say this because he was so taken by the beauty of Jesus' life. He wrote of 'the gentle figure of Christ, so patient, so kind, so loving, so full of forgiveness . . . it was a beautiful example, I thought, of the perfect man'.[3] Jesus was 'non-violence par excellence'.[4] Indeed, he went so far as to say that the Spirit of Jesus was the only spirit that could save India.

Jewish people, of course, have suffered much at the hands of an ill-thought-out Christian faith that failed to appreciate the Jewishness of Jesus and colluded with the prejudices of earlier times. This meant that Jewish references to Jesus were often unfriendly. From the nineteenth century onwards, however, a number of Jewish scholars have sought to re-establish the Jewish credentials of Jesus, Geza Vermes chief among them with his *Jesus the Jew*[5] and his studies of the Passion and resurrection of Jesus. The Jewish philosopher Martin Buber wrote, 'I have found in Jesus my great brother'.[6] Hopefully there is more to come in this scholarly dialogue.

Not surprisingly perhaps, the Dalai Lama focuses on the ethical teaching of the Sermon on the Mount. He compares Jesus' demanding saying that we should love our enemy with the Buddhist text, 'If you do not practise compassion towards your enemy then towards whom can you practise it?' Sikhism is inclined to find good in many faithful places so perhaps it's not surprising to find a Sikh ashram outside Delhi with a 'Jesus place' where Jesus is said to have appeared to its founder.

In other words, Jesus has friends in many different religions. So then, what do we make of key Gospel texts such as John 14.6, 'I am the way, and the truth, and the life. No-one comes to the Father except through me'?

The uniqueness of Christ

I am passionate about Jesus Christ. I want everyone to know about him and to be attracted to his extraordinary life and to try and follow his superb guidance about living well. Not to share that good news would be like discovering that holy grail, a cure for cancer, and filing it away for future reference. But deeper than my passion for Christ I probably need a passion for the truth. After all, if Jesus was not telling the truth about God and about human life I would be deluded to cling to his vision of the truth, and I would be a false guide if I commended his way to others. Truth has to have my highest loyalty.

And this is where I hit the road-block, because while I see the truth in Jesus, other perfectly rational and genuinely good people see the truth in other shapes and sizes, whether that be the teachings of Muhammad or the Buddha, or the way of life characteristic of Hindus or Sikhs, or even the practices of Wicca or Humanism. Respect for the integrity of others and humility before my own limitations compel me to agree with Oliver Cromwell who famously said, 'In the bowels of Christ, consider it possible you may be mistaken.' As my wife tells me, it has been known.

Before tackling that fundamental problem, however, I want to offer a reminder that faith truly lived, in whatever form, is usually deeply impressive. What disconcerts the unbeliever is often not the arguments of believers but their lives. The veteran film-maker Antony Thomas made a film for Channel 4 in 2009 called *Revelations*. In it he interviewed the Archbishop of Canterbury, Rowan Williams, the Archbishop of Westminster, Vincent Nichols, the Chief Rabbi, Jonathan Sacks, Muslim scholar, Tariq Ramadan, and Hindu holy man, Sadhu Paramtattvadas. He bombarded them with impossible questions but afterwards he concluded, 'Our five religious thinkers are among the most engaging, intelligent, honest and compassionate men it has ever been my privilege to meet.'[7] I was not surprised to hear that. However, Thomas then went on, 'The surprise is how much closer they are to each other than to many who claim to share their beliefs.' Yes, maybe so, but they are certainly not saying what so many people would like to believe – that their great faith traditions are all saying the same thing *really*.

Compare and contrast?

'No-one comes to the Father except through me.' That is the great stumbling block which has beset the relations of Christians with people of other faiths. There seems to be an explicit arrogance in that approach in which some Christians have gloried and in which others have winced. One way of dealing with the issue has been to claim that Christianity is not simply one faith among others but rather the end of religion. Christ stands over against all faiths as the one who negated religion as the human attempt to reach after God. Rather, the argument goes, God has now irrevocably reached after humankind. The initiative has been entirely the other way, and religion is therefore rendered redundant. Whereas in other faiths we have been looking for living water, in Christ the living water has come looking for us. There is a respectable theological pedigree for that approach but it still assumes the unlikely and arrogant position that only in Christ has God been reaching out to the world of human beings. It makes the assumption that all the genius of other faiths has been so much human dross, the mistaken construction of religious systems. Moreover, purely at the level of religion as a human phenomenon, Christianity has to be placed on some kind of theological or anthropological map.

Three approaches have often been outlined in recent years. One is called the *exclusivist* approach and it makes the bold claim that unless someone is able to say explicitly that 'Jesus is Lord' then that person cannot be ultimately acceptable to God. Such an approach posits an impossibly harsh view of God such that the vast majority of human beings, whether they have had the opportunity to hear of Jesus or not, would be refused entry to God's kingdom. This is not a God many of us would want to spend much time with.

A second approach is called *pluralist* because it maintains that although the great world faiths differ in content and practice, they are all on a similar footing in relation to ultimate truth, with none 'better' than another and none more qualified to have saving quality than another. This is clearly attractive to a culture where choice is the highest social value, but it bypasses the knotty issue of truth, and confounds hundreds of millions of adherents of religion who clearly have passionate beliefs about the meaning and efficacy of their own faith tradition. They simply do not see syncretism as a helpful strategy but look rather for a deeper manner of engagement.

Yet another approach employed by Christians goes under the name of *inclusivist* because it seeks to recognize the presence of Christ in other faiths wherever the character of Christ is shown. Thus, where grace, forgiveness, love, compassion, a hunger for justice and a commitment to peace-making are present, there it could be said are echoes of the Divine Stranger who embodied these values in his life and death. So Christ saves from within the living structure of other faiths. The problem with this otherwise attractive approach is that it colonizes other faiths by making their adherents 'anonymous Christians'. They simply don't wish to be 'anonymous' anything; they want to be visible, authentic members of their own faith tradition ('thank you very much!').

But still Jesus challenges us: 'No-one comes to the Father except through me.' So what is to be done?

One approach is to suggest that no-one comes to God *as a loving Father* except those who have seen God in the person of Jesus. Only Christianity has this particular understanding of the nature of God. While there is an element of truth in this, adherents of Judaism and Islam, for example, might protest that they too have this understanding, among other images of God. In which case the difference is one of emphasis rather than essence.

A better theological starting point is to be found in the concept of the 'logos' which was familiar to both Greek and Jew at the time of Jesus. To the Greek mind the logos is the creative, ordering principle behind the universe. To the Jewish mind the logos is the creative Word of God which could not go forth from God without achieving its goal. The logos 'enlightens everyone' (John 1.9) and there are demonstrations and outcroppings of the logos, therefore, in every faith and culture. God's truth is not confined to any discrete religious box; it ranges wild and free over the whole of creation. Theologian Austin Farrer wrote,

> Faith perishes if it is walled in or confined. If it is anywhere, it must be everywhere, like God himself . . . You must be able

to spread your recognition of him, and the basis of your conviction about him, as widely as your thought will range.[8]

Christians, of course, believe that the logos is seen spectacularly and fully in the person of Jesus, but that doesn't need to stop them recognizing the Special Presence in other places too. The particular value of this approach is that it maintains a belief in the universal purposes of God and his mission of love. God can be no-one's possession, nor confined to any system of thought. It's important that we settle for nothing less.

The place of dialogue

If that theology informs and supports our relations with people of other faiths, then what are the appropriate, respectful and yet authentic styles of engagement? A Vatican document, *Dialogue and Proclamation*, in 1991 spoke of four areas of dialogue.

- *Dialogue of life.* In many parts of the country, but particularly in places such as Bradford, Burnley, Leicester, London and the like, there are churches and mosques, churches and gurdwaras, churches and temples, facing each other across busy urban streets. The dialogue of life happens where people from each faith community visit and befriend each other, support each other in time of need and encourage each other in worship and pastoral care. It's happening.
- *Dialogue of action.* There are times when faith communities need to act together in the face of injustice and pain or when there is a common goal in the flourishing of the wider community through a particular social project. These are lovely opportunities for joint action, with hard work and, happily, much eating.
- *Dialogue of theological exchange.* This takes place when there is clear agreement that the beliefs of the respective communities are to come under the spotlight. It's an opportunity for respectful listening and learning, and for sharing the passions that excite us in our faith. This can be open and free, and the result

may be an exhilarating exchange which truly opens eyes and minds. With such exchange comes the risk of deeper transformation, with movement in both directions. It's evangelism without angularity, witness without pressure.

- *Dialogue of religious experience.* This is one of the most rewarding areas of exchange because it reaches into the lived experience of someone's faith. This is where in honest conversation we share stories, convictions, practices, hopes and dreams. It's where we can name Jesus and his effect on our lives. It's where we get real.

Behind these dialogues is another contemporary reality worth acknowledging here. A bigger issue than our religious differences is often the solidarity we experience as faith communities today in our relationship with the rest of society. For all people of faith, religion is a major, defining reality. It gives us an identity and a framework of values in which all else is lived, and so the prevailing secularism and religious illiteracy in society is something we all face as a common and continuing problem. That which unites us is then truly greater than that which divides us. The secular assumption that there is no transcendence and no finality is leading to a major conflict over the place of religion in the public square. There are arguments over religious dress, faith schools, the celebration of festivals, the acceptability of offering to pray for people, ethical issues about the beginning and end of life, and so on. And here the Church of England is often seen by leaders of other faith communities as the gatekeeper for all. Far from resenting the place of the Anglican Church in the life of the nation, many faith leaders applaud it. This doesn't negate the differences between the major faiths in our country but it does relativize them in the face of the deeper conflict we have over the nature of reality itself.

So what about evangelism?

Talk of dialogue will immediately cause some Christians to smell a rat. They fear that the gospel is being sold out to what they see as a soft, liberal alternative and that the uniqueness of Christ is being disowned. 'What about the Great Commission?' they say. 'Make disciples of all nations, baptizing them in the name of the Father and of the Son and of the Holy Spirit' (Matt. 28.19). That's foundational in Christian mission; it's not up for renegotiation. Leaving aside the question of whether Jesus could actually have spoken in such a complete Trinitarian form at that time, that commission has undoubtedly been a key motivator for the startlingly successful mission of the Church over these 2,000 years, and has seen the Church grow from the handful gathered around Jesus at the Ascension to the two billion Christians around the world today.

I happily sign up to that commission. I want to share what has been wonderfully good news in my own experience with anyone who shows any interest in hearing it. Nevertheless, I am clear about what is permissible in a multi-faith world and what is unacceptable. I can share my story and my understanding of Christ to the limit of my ability, but I must do this in interfaith encounter with the utmost respect for the delight believers from other faith traditions have in their own way of truth and life.

The Christian Muslim Forum has helpfully produced a set of guidelines for Christian and Muslim witness in the UK, and the wisdom of these ground rules can be applied to the whole field of interfaith encounter. They start with the recognition that 'we bear witness to, and proclaim our faith, not only through words but through our attitudes, actions and lifestyles'. Who we are speaks as loudly as what we say – indeed more so. As Jesus said, 'You will know them by their fruits' (Matt. 7.16). The guidelines continue with perhaps the most important statement of all, that 'we cannot convert people, only God can do that. In our language and methods we should recognize that people's choice of faith is primarily a matter between themselves and God.' How refreshing it would be if all evangelism was conducted in that humble spirit, where God is the evangelist and we chip in where we can.

The guidelines go on with similar wisdom. Sharing our faith should not be coercive or manipulative or linked with any inducement. We should 'speak of our faith without demeaning or ridiculing the faith of others'. We should respect the decisions converts make and not harass them – and so on. These are all sane, wise ground rules. They don't require any sacrifice of the burning belief we have in the vitality and preciousness of the gospel. They simply require us to recognize that others feel the same about entirely different faiths, and that they deserve the respect and courtesy we ourselves would expect. I remember as a young Christian hearing a sermon on the courtesy of Christ and instinctively knowing that this was a very important lesson to carry with me through life. I try to follow it still.

The secret lies in finding that point where boldness and respect are held in a generous balance. I hear it in Archbishop John Sentamu's lovely greeting to fellow faith leaders, 'I greet you in the name of Jesus, who to you is a prophet and to me is a Saviour.' Here is both clarity and humility, holy joy and warm invitation. It is something like this that we seek in all Christian witness in an interfaith context. Jesus is to be named without fear, but our ears are to be open to words of similar conviction from others.

One of the basic questions for Christians to ask themselves is, 'How confident am I in the loving truth of Jesus Christ?' If God is as we have seen him in Jesus then we enter dialogue with nothing to fear. Let God be God and all shall be well. I know that a saving knowledge of God is to be found in Jesus. I don't know about other ways – though I believe that 'in [the logos] was life, and the life was the light of all people' (John 1.4). I simply share what I know.

Isn't that enough?

11

Jesus – to the end of time

The story is told of young Wolfgang Mozart going out one evening with his friends and returning late at night in high spirits after his father Leopold had gone to bed. Mozart mischievously went to the harpsichord in the salon and loudly played a scale – but omitting the final note. Leopold heard this and desperately tried to go back to sleep, but always that final note cried out to be played. The frustration was unbearable. Eventually he gave up. Wearily he went downstairs, walked over to the harpsichord and played the final, deeply satisfying note. Then he went back to bed.

There is in every part of human experience a deep need to complete. Every narrative looks for some kind of resolution. Every book needs an ending; every film needs rounding off; every life seeks a good death. How much more, then, does the greatest narrative of all, the story of the world (or the meta-narrative of the universe), need proper completion. It is this that Paul writes of in Ephesians when he says,

> he has made known to us the mystery of his will, according to his good pleasure that he set forth in Christ, as a plan for the fullness of time, to gather up all things in him, things in heaven and things on earth. (Eph. 1.9, 10)

Paul clearly sees Jesus Christ as the key to the end of all things, just as 'all things came into being through him' (John 1.3) at the beginning, and just as he has been present at the centre of history throughout time (see Chapter 3). The 'final note' will be Jesus.

The medium-term future

We will return to this later, but what about the medium term? What might happen to the story of Jesus in the coming decades and centuries? He has clearly been the most influential figure in human history so far, but will that continue? It's hard to say, of course. There are so many huge shifts taking place in the global village. In the West, much to the concern of the churches, the Christian story is disappearing from our culture. A MORI poll in 2007 found that only 56 per cent of those surveyed believed in God, though belief in hell and guardian angels was increasing. The British Social Attitudes Survey in 2004 found 43 per cent of people saying they had no religion. *The Mail on Sunday* reported that 43 per cent of the population of the UK had no idea what happened at Easter. In many younger parts of society all that remains is a vague hotch-potch of phrases without any known points of reference – 'Good Samaritan', 'Prodigal Son', 'Judas', even 'crucifixion' (though 'a woman caught in adultery' may have more resonance).

One of the consequences of this loss of the story is that it makes us a society of what might be called 'absolute beginners'. It's always dangerous when a society forgets where it has come from because it's then prone either to repeat the mistakes of the past or to have to invent itself all over again – its basic values, its moral and political ground rules, its self-understanding and so on. This is an exhausting process and open to all sorts of extremism as powerful groups seek to take over unoccupied ground. An unthinking secularism tends to dismiss the sure Christian foundations of Western culture, including its influence on political democracy, liberal education, scientific enterprise, social justice, communitarian values, artistic creativity, and so much more. Playwright and atheist John Mortimer once wrote to the *Daily Telegraph* to say: 'Our whole history and culture in Europe is based on Christianity, whether you believe in it or not. Our culture is Christian; Shakespeare, Mozart – all that makes life worth living is part of the Christian tradition.'[1] For each generation to try and start again is folly. 'Absolute beginners' are dangerous.

Alongside this loss of the Christian story is another paradoxical phenomenon – the newly recognized significance of religion on the global scene. The twentieth-century disciples of secularism, Communism, anarchism and similar ideologies who were happily predicting the demise of religion within a few decades would have been shocked to see how central to contemporary political and social debate the place of religion has become. This has not always been for the reasons men and women of faith would have wanted, of course, and there is much unhealthy, violent and repressive religion which needs to be reformed. Nevertheless, former Prime Minister Tony Blair said in March 2009,

> As the years of my premiership passed, one fact struck me with increasing force: that failure to understand the power of religion meant failure to understand the modern world. Religious faith and how it develops could be of the same significance to the 21st century as political ideology was to the 20th.[2]

A book by the editors of *The Economist* magazine in 2009 was entitled *God is Back*. Indeed so. For good or ill, no-one in leadership today can afford to ignore the influence of faith.

The problem with this resurgence of interest in things religious, however, is that it coincides with quite serious religious illiteracy among those who have to handle the political and social implications of resurgent religion. This applies both at governmental level and perhaps even more so in the corridors of local government, where mechanistic readings of procedures and regulations combine with one-eyed readings of religious belief and practice. The result is constant irritation on all sides. Renaming Christmas 'Winterval' is just one example of the crazy excesses of political correctness in the field of religion. The situation is not helped by a desire in secular authority to treat all religious groups together as a single entity of 'faith communities' with an ill-defined syncretistic belief in Something Different. The result is that incomprehension abounds.

A further cultural shift in the West has been the emergence of a more confident, aggressive atheism expressed in the robust

writings of Richard Dawkins, Christopher Hitchens and Daniel
Dennett, and in the novels of Philip Pullman and others. It sometimes seems that an essential first statement in interviews with the
famous is, 'I no longer believe in God, but . . .' – as in Julian Barnes'
introduction to his BBC Lent series in 2008, 'I don't believe in
God, but I miss him.' Or Poet Laureate Andrew Motion, when
interviewed by *The Guardian* in 2009, who said first of all, 'I'm
not a believer,' but added that his love of the Bible remains: 'It's
about the power of these words to connect with deep, recurring
human truths.'[3] (By contrast I rather like Ian Hislop's modest
definition of himself as a 'failed agnostic'.) The effect of this more
open expression of atheism in the media has been the quite swift
emergence of a default position of unbelief in wider society. This
isn't necessarily a well-thought-out intellectual position, more an
instinctive response to the way the cultural wind is blowing. For
some it allows more honesty; for others it's just an easier ride.

A counter-cultural narrative

The effect of these broad cultural shifts is potentially quite exhilarating for Christians. They allow the story of Jesus once again to
be a great counter-cultural narrative, set against the prevailing
secular (and post-secular) wisdom of the times. This is how the
wild story of a crucified and risen Saviour first entered the Greek
and Roman world. In a culture of gods and godlessness the extraordinary story of Jesus sounded an utterly new and refreshing note.
The world was intrigued. It said, 'We will to hear you again about
this . . .' (Acts 17.32). The result was the explosion of Christianity
all over the globe.

The rediscovered secret should be the importance of 'difference',
the Christian difference in every department of life. Truly following the way of Jesus gives Christians a wonderful mandate to be
radically different. There was a remarkably clear demonstration
of this in an edition of the magazine *The Week*. On the same page
were two stories. One was of Karl Lagerfeld, creative director of
Chanel for nearly 30 years. He was quoted as saying,

I take a physical pleasure in revenge, often in a vicious way, and I'll wait as long as it takes to pay back anyone who has wronged me. When people think it is all forgotten, I pull the chair away – maybe ten years later. They do not even know it is me who in the end kills them. I am very dangerous for that. Do not touch me – I will most definitely touch you.

The other story was of a young Tutsi in Rwanda at the time of the genocide in 1994. Immaculee Iligabaiza, a devout Catholic, was 22 when she lost her entire family. As the violence broke out she took refuge with a Protestant pastor. When order had been restored three months later she found her father had been shot, her mother hacked to death and her brother caught in a crowd that had been sprayed with machine-gun bullets. The leader of this savagery had been a local businessman who Immaculee knew; she had even played with his children at school. Believing it was what her family would have expected of her, she resolved to visit him in prison. 'He was sobbing,' she said. 'I could feel his shame. I reached out, touched his hands and said what I'd come to say: "I forgive you."'[4]

This is the kind of difference that being a follower of Jesus encourages. We don't all achieve that level of behaviour, but we aspire to it and we set it before the world as an alternative. I encountered another dimension of that alternative way of life in the outskirts of Cairo a few years ago when I visited the suburb of Mukatam, where the whole community is given over to sorting through the rubbish of Cairo. You can imagine the smell. We arrived in a small luxury coach. When I saw the poverty there I feared the worst, or at least I feared the odd stone thrown in protest at these voyeurs in their smart transport. Very soon, however, I noticed that in nearly all the ground-floor garages open to the street, where the rubbish was being sorted, there were also large posters of Jesus, Mary and the saints. As we threaded our way through the streets in our coach, everywhere there were smiles and waves. We were welcome. On the craggy hillside above the settlement were massive carvings of the resurrection, the Ascension and Christ in glory. We were taken to a huge open church carved out of the mountainside which we were told would hold 30,000 people. The evening we were there was a minor feast day for a saint I forget, so they expected 'only' about 6–7,000 people at Mass. Here again was the Christian difference. In the midst of hard and unpleasant work there wasn't misery but glory. The people were gloriously alive, seeking to better their community and finding hope in their faith.

What we have, therefore, is a great opportunity for Christians to put forward the story of Jesus as a great counter-cultural narrative, and also an opportunity for Christian communities to be seen as distinctive, attractive alternatives to the atomized, self-assertive lifestyles of today. There are few places in our culture where people of wide differences in age, background, wealth, education, employment, leisure interests, and so forth, can meet and enjoy genuine encounter and mutual enrichment (the usual word is 'fellowship'), while at the same time gathering around deeply important issues, both locally and internationally. The Church has been 'doing community' for a very long time and knows a thing or two that governments have been trying to discover for decades. Now at last, in the clean, refreshing air of our unbelieving, baffled culture, we have the chance to make the promise of a vibrant counter-cultural community come true.

There's just one problem – we will have to put aside our small ambitions and our narrow, internal arguments. We will need to leave behind our tribal loyalties to the particular banners of church tradition and theological preference that we habitually wave at one another. We will have instead to declare simply that we are 'followers of Jesus'. And we will have to follow Jesus very closely, very closely indeed.

Jesus to the end of time

We have been looking at the middle distance and what significance Jesus might have in the next decades and centuries, but I have boldly claimed that Jesus is the centre of history and that he holds the field to the end of time, that his is the 'final note'. What does that mean?

The beginning and the end of the biblical story is told in pictorial language. The truth-telling story of the Garden of Eden and the mixed fortunes of our mythical ancestors at the start is balanced at the end by the picture of the new Jerusalem 'coming down out of heaven from God' (Rev. 21.2) and the 'river of the water of life . . . flowing from the throne of God . . . through the middle of the street of the city' (Rev 22.1, 2). We are given a picture of God finally dwelling with his people and wiping every tear from their eye (Rev. 21.3, 4). It's a picture we have long loved and by which we have been much comforted. But what on earth (or heaven) does it mean?

Well, actually, it probably means something for both earth and heaven, but first we need to recognize that we are in the arena of theological language and that this discourse is distinct from scientific or cosmological language. Those conversant with the latter languages tell us that ultimately either all matter could collapse into black holes or that, through the Big Crunch, matter and space-time could collapse into a dimensionless singularity. Of course, human life will come to an end much sooner than that, and tragically it may happen pre-emptively through our own madness as we pollute and exhaust the planet or as we blow each other out of existence. Pray for greater wisdom.

But what do these scientific scenarios mean theologically? This isn't the place for a full exploration of the fascinating range of theological possibilities but we can at least revisit what we noted earlier, that Ephesians is quite clear that God will 'gather up all things in him, things in heaven and things on earth' (Eph. 1.10). In Colossians Paul points again to the supremacy of Christ in God's purposes: 'through him [Christ] God was pleased to reconcile to himself all things, whether on earth or in heaven, by making peace through the blood of his cross' (Col. 1.20). (I can feel the words flowing over my head even as I type – let's try and halt the flow for once and think what they mean!) The picture we have of the end of the age from these texts is of *all things being gathered together in Christ, and Christ finally being revealed in all his glory*. In 1 Corinthians 15 Paul sees every authority in the cosmos being brought into subjection to Jesus Christ, including the final enemy, death itself. Then Christ will hand over the kingdom to God – job done – and God will be 'all in all' (1 Cor. 15.28).

The second coming of Christ (not often referred to as such in the New Testament) is therefore the revealing of Christ as utterly and majestically present to his world, in a way that has been hidden since his first coming. And this revealing of Christ to the world will usher in the new creation (Rom. 8.19–21), of which we've seen the first instalment in the resurrection of Jesus. He has been present in his Spirit since Pentecost, but when the time comes he will be present in all his fullness and the new world order that he inaugurated in his ministry will be established for ever. The new creation, the 'new Jerusalem', will come down out of heaven from God, prepared as a bride for her husband (Rev. 21.2). Heaven and earth will be joined for ever. Truly a marriage made in heaven.

Now, this is a tight theological argument, and is necessarily drawn in picture, metaphor and poetry. It needs much more space to consider properly, but at the very least it tells us that the new creation is not an unearthly ideal but is a this-worldly reality, and when Jesus told us to pray 'your kingdom come on earth' he really meant it. New creation is for this world, not for a distant heaven. Which would seem to mean that this universe belongs to God, who has revealed his love for it in Jesus Christ, and at the end he is not going to screw it up like a useless piece of paper and throw it away. The universe matters; the earth matters; you and I matter. Our identity now and our security in the future are to be found in God, the One who will be 'all in all'. And the guarantee and foretaste of that transformation, that new creation, are clearly seen in the resurrection of Jesus Christ.

In the meantime . . .

It might be a good spiritual discipline to live each day as if it is our last (or first), but in the meantime there is a lot to be done. We have to get on with preparing the world for the Great Event, the revealing of the presence of Christ and his new creation. To reduce this idea to a manageable concept: a newly married couple are likely to work quite hard to clean up their house before a visit from the in-laws. They want it to be ready. We too want the world to be as ready as we can make it before the Coming–Revealing of Christ. Like the house, we know it's a bit of a mess; we know it has rubbish lying around; we know there are parts of it that haven't had a clean since we arrived. More importantly, we know our world is full of injustice and need. It needs a clean-up.

Here lies the political and social agenda I wrote about in Chapter 5. In his ministry Jesus was already announcing the arrival of the kingdom of God, the start of the gathering in of all things ready for the new creation. So Christians, of all people, have an irresistible motivation to get involved in political and social action because they know it's the task of getting the world ready for its final make-over. And nothing is too small to contribute to the task. When President Kennedy visited the Space Center where they were planning the Apollo space launches he met a man with a broom and a bucket. 'What do you do?' asked the President. 'I'm helping to get a man on the moon,' said the man, proudly. Every contribution makes a difference in the great task of preparing for the kingdom.

A teacher encourages and shapes the young lives in her care to value truthful enquiry and honest character. A not-so-young couple faithfully turn out every Sunday night to nurture a small group of teenagers in their stumbling faith. A loyal group of women provide lunch and friendship every Wednesday for 25 or so older residents of their village. A young mum hasn't got much time to offer but she mentors a young person who keeps getting into trouble. An elderly couple give sacrificially to a range of charities as well as writing letters to political and religious prisoners for Amnesty International. These are the small actions that prepare the ground for God's coming kingdom. Other Christians are in positions of greater influence and can press for ethical changes in financial practices, or bold legislative responses to the challenge of climate change, or more generosity to desperate asylum seekers. Some Christians, moreover, are called to leadership and know that discipleship costs real intellectual, emotional and spiritual effort. The general point, however, is that each one of us is a potential partner in God's big agenda for a new world, the new creation heralded by Jesus.

Yesterday, today and for ever

Jesus is the plot, the sub-plot, the chapter headings and the footnotes of Christianity. Moreover, the story of Jesus continues to haunt the world with its humility, majesty and truth. People may dismiss the Church but they rarely dismiss Jesus. Jesus is the transforming presence at the heart of the Church and of a vast number of lives. With the Church globally increasing at the rate of over 70,000 a day it seems that nothing can stop Jesus attracting people to himself. He turns round lives that are lost and in pain. He inspires projects and programmes of social reform worldwide. He causes people to live and die heroically. He is the best that humankind has ever been and the joy of 'man's' desiring. He is the same yesterday, today and for ever, and so he draws us from who we were once, to who we are now, and towards who we shall be one day.

Spike Milligan lived and died as a great comedian, but shortly before his death he wrote a foreword for a book called *The Good God Guide*. In it he said:

> As a lad I was very religious, much moved by the life and death of Jesus. I prayed to him every night and went to mass every Sunday. Now I'm ancient and don't go to church any more (the conscience still twitches a bit as a result) but I'm basically a Jesus man, still.[5]

'A Jesus man' is about as good a goal as I can hope to achieve in this life. I shall count it a privilege to stay in Jesus' good company for all my time ahead, until I too hear that 'final note'. And I believe that note will be played, and played perfectly, by the Master Musician himself – Jesus, who came that I might have life, and have it more abundantly than I ever dreamed possible.

GROUP STUDY COURSE

What follows is material to enable a group to dig for themselves into the life and meanings of Jesus. There are sessions for each chapter of the book, so the first thing to say is – don't use them all! The group leader can decide which sessions would be most appropriate for that particular group in the number of sessions available. A judicious choice of, say, three or four studies could be just as satisfying as six or eight. Indeed, material could be pulled out for a study day or a church weekend.

It is clearly very beneficial if everyone has read the chapter during the week prior to the session.

The format used is as follows:

An *anchor passage* is identified.

Way in

Attentive listening and reflection on the passage is encouraged by keeping a solid period of silence. A minute is a surprisingly long time to those who aren't used to it, but the length of time should be judged in relation to the nature of the group. Two or three minutes might eventually be none too long. There follows an introductory question which draws on the experience of the group and sets the scene for the particular study. Note that one session – 'In the mind of the artist' – requires asking the group *the week before* to bring something with them the following week.

Way through

These questions take the group into the meat of the chapter being discussed, ending with a question relating directly to the anchor passage. Depending on the nature of the group, further questions from the anchor passage might be prepared.

Way forward

This question is designed to take the group out of the study into some form of personal or corporate action arising out of it.

Deeper

This is an opportunity for prayerful response to the study, usually involving some short activity, a collect (special prayer), the Lord's Prayer (note the suggestion in 'Changing the rules' and 'The world's hope'), and a final V and R (versicle and response). The last session involves singing!

Preparation

Sometimes there is need for some minor preparation of, say, pictures of Jesus, paper and pen, newspapers, candles, night-lights, large paper and scissors, a world map, stones, music to play, music to sing.

This material is of course only indicative. It can be adjusted entirely as the leader thinks best for the group.

Jesus – a personal obsession

Anchor passage: 1 John 1.1–4

Way in

- Read the anchor passage and keep a full minute's silence (or more) to reflect on it.
- What are your earliest memories of Jesus?

Way through

- Do you recognize any of the pictures of Jesus mentioned by the author (Gentle Jesus, Judge Jesus, etc.; pp. 2–9) in your own experience? [Use an array of pictures and paintings as further prompts if you have them available in books, cards, posters, etc.]
- Do you have a favourite image of Jesus? Where do you think that image comes from? Where does it connect with the picture of Jesus in the Gospels?
- What do you think most people in the UK think of Jesus today? What might be the points of connection between their lives and values and the life and values of Jesus?
- *Anchor passage*: 1 John 1.1–4. John's amazement at having been so close to 'the word of life' shines through this passage. What is it about Jesus that 'amazes' you and that you would want to pass on to a sceptical world?

Way forward

The blogger on page 11 writes of how uncomfortable following Jesus can be. Where do you find following Jesus most demanding?

Deeper

The leader recapitulates some of the images of Jesus mentioned in the discussion and gives space to give thanks or to reflect silently on each one. 'We give thanks for "Professor Jesus" and the work of biblical scholars . . .' 'We're aware of how many of us carry

"Judge Jesus" around in our heads, and we ask to be released from that image . . .'

Collect

Lord Jesus Christ
your birth at Bethlehem
draws us to kneel in wonder at heaven touching earth:
accept our heartfelt praise
as we worship you
our Saviour and our eternal God.

The Lord's Prayer

V. Let us bless the Lord. R. Thanks be to God.

Jesus – the magnificent outsider

Anchor passage: Matthew 5.38–48

Way in

- Read the anchor passage and keep a full minute's silence (or more) to reflect on it.
- In 'The basic facts' at the start of the chapter (p. 16), are there any statements that surprise you or that you want to discuss further?

Way through

- In the section on Jesus the subversive (p. 20), it's said that Jesus didn't believe in badges. What are the badges worn both in society and in the Church to which Jesus might take exception today?
- Which of the Beatitudes do you find it hardest to believe? How do you reconcile the Beatitudes with reality?
- 'The meaning of the miracles is more important than their historicity' (p. 28). Do you agree, and if so, what is their meaning, then and now?
- *Anchor passage*: Matthew 5.38–48. 'But I say to you . . .' Was he serious? How should we understand these demanding standards today?

Way forward

At its simplest, Christians are followers of Jesus. (See Rob Bell quote on p. 31.) So what will that mean tomorrow in the specific settings in which each member of the group will find themselves? What difference will it make?

Deeper

The leader gives out small pieces of paper and pens: 'What one thing has struck you afresh about being a follower of Jesus? Write that down . . . Now let's offer those thoughts to God in silence, and ask for grace to live like that tomorrow . . . Now put that piece of paper in your pocket or handbag and put it some-where visible at home as a reminder that you're going to try and live like that.'

Collect

Eternal God
whose Son went among the crowds
and brought healing with his touch:
help us to show his love
in your Church as we gather together
and by our lives as they are transformed
into the image of Christ our Lord.

The Lord's Prayer

V. Let us bless the Lord. R. Thanks be to God.

Jesus – centre point of history

Anchor passage: Hebrews 1.1–4

Way in

- Read the anchor passage and keep a full minute's silence (or more) to reflect on it.
- Who else, apart from Jesus, can claim to have truly revolutionized the ways of the world? Try and justify those claims to the rest of the group, whose task it is to be sceptical.
- Now do the same with Jesus: one person justify the claim, others be sceptical.

Way through

- Are the Jordan Management Consultants fair on the disciples (p. 34)? Could you make an alternative case?
- The coming of Jesus was a definitive 'kairos' moment (p. 38). In what sense could it be said that the Church is in a kairos moment today?
- 'The gospel is often like a slow-burning fuse' (p. 41). Is that sufficient to justify some of the dark episodes in Christian history?
- *Anchor passage*: Hebrews 1.1–4. What does it mean to speak of a Son 'through whom he also created the worlds' (v. 2)? And how would you explain to an unchurched person what is meant by 'He is the reflection of God's glory, and the exact imprint of God's very being' (v. 3)?

Way forward

The ordinand said, 'I still need to turn to Christ every day as if it was for the first time' (p. 43). In practical terms, what might that mean?

Deeper

Light a large central candle representing Christ the Light of the world. Give each person a night-light and ask them to light it from the Christ candle (with a taper) and to place it wherever they want it to be in relation to the Christ candle. The group does this in silence and holds that silence for reflection and prayer.

Collect

Lord Jesus Christ
light of the nations and glory of Israel
make your home among us
and present us pure and holy
to your heavenly Father
your God, and our God.

The Lord's Prayer

V. Let us bless the Lord. R. Thanks be to God.

Jesus – changing the rules

Anchor passage: Luke 4.14–21

Way in

- Read the anchor passage and keep a full minute's silence to reflect on it.
- Have copies of some of the week's newspapers. Look at the headlines. What would be a Christian response to some of those issues?

Way through

- Is there too much special Christian pleading in the sections on 'Facing the world with compassion' (p. 45) and 'Confronting the structures' (p. 48)?
- What are the issues in society at present that you think deserve more attention from the Church?
- *Anchor passage*: Luke 4.14–21. Who were 'the captives' to whom Jesus was proclaiming release, and who are they for us today? Similarly, who were and are 'the blind'?

Way forward

If your church were to offer more of a *contrast* as a Christian community (p. 51) what would need to happen?

Deeper

List on a large piece of paper the places and groups in the local community that are doing the work of Christ in compassion and bringing about change. Then pray for them out loud or in silence. Each person could choose which one to pray for especially, promising also to pray for that place or group every day in the coming week. (Cut up the piece of paper and give the name of the place or group to the group member as a reminder.)

Collect

God of all mercy
your Son proclaimed good news to the poor
release to the captives
and freedom to the oppressed:
anoint us with your Holy Spirit
and set all your people free
to praise you in Christ our Lord.

The Lord's Prayer (try pausing for a time at 'your kingdom come' before completing the prayer).

V. Let us bless the Lord. R. Thanks be to God.

Jesus – the world's hope

Anchor passage: Luke 4.22–30

Way in

- Read the anchor passage and keep a full minute's silence to reflect on it.
- What are your three greatest concerns for this country and the wider world at present? Have you done anything about any of them (however small) or have you felt powerless?

Way through

- 'Unrestrained consumption and a rapidly exhausted environment' (p. 59) is presented in this chapter as a toxic combination with potentially catastrophic consequences. Is this scaremongering?
- Is Jesus' alternative framing story of the kingdom of the Common Good (p. 60) a realistic option in the hard world of today? Does Bono's challenge (p. 61) ring true?
- How workable is Jesus' kingdom of Intentional Peace (p. 66) in a world of naked terrorism and global jihad?
- *Anchor passage*: Luke 4.22–30. Prophets have a hard time at home. Has the contemporary Church lost its prophetic voice?

Way forward

In the light of this discussion, what one thing could you do, and what one further thing could your church do, to see forward the alternative framing story of the kingdom of God?

Deeper

Lay out a map of the world with one large candle in the corner and a number of small night-lights around the edge. Invite group members to light their night-light from the Christ candle (with a taper) and put it on a country in the world where there is particular need. That person can then name the problem and keep silence for prayer, or pray audibly in his or her own way for that place. Summing-up prayer from the leader.

Collect

Risen Christ
your wounds declare your love for the world
and the wonder of your risen life:
give us compassion and courage
to risk ourselves for those we serve
to the glory of God the Father.

The Lord's Prayer (try pausing again at 'your kingdom come' – it might come more easily this time).

V. Let us bless the Lord. R. Thanks be to God.

Jesus – crazy about the Church

Anchor passage: 1 Peter 2.4–10

Way in

- Read the anchor passage and keep a full minute's silence to reflect on it.
- If you were to describe your church as a type of animal or bird, what would it be? And why? (Trust this strange request – it works!)

Way through

- 'The Church is simply those who have been immersed in, soaked in, the life of Jesus, and who have been invited to eat with him and pray to the Father with him' (p. 69). Does this definition appeal to you? What might be missing?
- How should the practices of the early Church influence the practices of the Church today? Or: how do we balance the normative nature of biblical practice with the Spirit-led development of the Church through the centuries?
- If you were describing to someone who isn't a Christian what the Eucharist means to you, what would you say?
- *Anchor passage*: 1 Peter 2.4–10. If we are being built into a spiritual house (v. 5) but now find ourselves living in a large number of separate houses, is it best to accept 'village living' or to still try to live in one big spiritual house? This could be applied both to the overall ecumenical scene or to the Anglican Communion.

Way forward

The Church in the West is undergoing a major sea-change. No longer is it business as usual, nor can Humpty Dumpty be put together again in the old way. What are the major building blocks the Church needs for its reconstruction? Or what are the main values by which it must live?

Deeper

Using the image of living stones, give each group member a stone to represent a section or activity of local church life. Alternatively the stones could represent different churches in the area. Build a cairn of these stones (or use a child's Lego to make a building) with group members praying for whatever the stone represents, either out loud or quietly. Give enough time for the prayer to be 'real'.

Collect

Gracious Father
revive the Church in our day
and make her holy, strong and faithful
for your glory's sake
in Jesus Christ our Lord.

The Lord's Prayer

V. Let us bless the Lord. R. Thanks be to God.

Jesus – partner in prayer

Anchor passage: Luke 11.1–10

Way in

- Read the anchor passage and keep a full minute's silence to reflect on it.
- What causes you to pray?
- Given that most of us feel that we don't pray very well at all, what or who has helped you most to make sense of prayer?

Way through

- Do you recognize the journey outlined in this chapter, from love at first sight, to second sight, then night sight, in-sight and maybe out-of-sight? Leader – go through the journey, asking group members if they would be prepared to share parts of their story at each stage.
- In particular, what has helped you to enrich your journey (second sight) and how have you coped with the dark periods (night sight)?
- Where does Jesus Christ figure in your praying?
- *Anchor passage*: Luke 11.1–10. It seems as if it's only because the man wears his friend down that the friend gets up to answer him. Can that be a true picture of God's responsiveness to our prayers? How does that sit with 'for everyone who knocks, the door will be opened'?

Way forward

What would help you to take the next step in praying, and who might help you?

Deeper

Experiment with silence. Take a full five minutes, or maybe more, inviting members of the group to be comfortable but alert, feet on the floor and hands in laps, open and waiting.

'Remember that Christ is gazing at you with love, here and now . . . ask for grace to let go of all that burdens you and to be open to his gift, however it may come . . . ask for the courage to return the gaze of Christ, little by little . . . when you need, silently repeat the phrase "My Lord and my God" . . . use that phrase to return to Christ, who awaits you always, with love . . .'

Come out of the silence gently with a prayer:

Almighty God,
you search us and know us:
may we rely on you in strength
and rest on you in weakness,
now and in all our days;
through Jesus Christ our Lord.

The Lord's Prayer

V. Let us bless the Lord. R. Thanks be to God.

Jesus – in a world of pain

Anchor passage: John 11.32–44

Way in

- Read the anchor passage and keep a full minute's silence to reflect on it. By now the group might want more time for this.
- 'Each of us carries a lot of pain of many different sorts. We need to be very sensitive to others and to ourselves in this session. Please only speak of what you feel able to share. And we can pause and take a break at any time. Having said that, when you look back at this last week or so, where have you been most conscious of the pain of the world, either in yourself or in the wider world?'

Way through

- We have probably all been both givers and receivers of compassion in time of need (p. 96). Has your experience of receiving been good? And how easy or difficult have you found it to offer compassion?
- The cross demonstrates that 'love, though defeated, is invincible' (p. 100). Have any of us experienced that?
- 'This is a God who ties one arm behind his back rather than force his will upon us' (p. 101). Would you rather he hadn't tied one arm behind his back? When is it appropriate to talk of these things (i.e. how to understand pain in relation to God) with someone who has been hurt by life or death?
- *Anchor passage*: John 11.32–44. Why do you think Jesus held back from coming to help Lazarus (v. 32)? How do you think the raising of Lazarus relates to the resurrection of Jesus?

Way forward

Is the Church a safe place for people to bring their pain? How can it be made safer and more a place of healing?

Deeper

Leader – on a tray or equivalent, mark out the shape of a cross in night-lights. Place the tray with the cross in the middle of the group, and invite group members to come and light the night-lights from a larger Christ candle, each light representing a particular person in pain. As the night-lights are lit, the name is said or a prayer offered. When the lights are all lit, read Romans 8.31–39.

Play some quiet or appropriate music e.g. 'I know that my Redeemer liveth' from *Messiah*, John Tavener's 'Song for Athene', Lauridsen's 'O magnum mysterium', Taizé 'Jesus, remember me' or 'Wait for the Lord'.

V. Let us bless the Lord. R. Thanks be to God.

Jesus – in the mind of the artist

Anchor passage: John 1.1–5, 14

Way in

- Read the anchor passage and keep a full minute's silence, or more, for reflection. 'God has incarnated, en-fleshed, himself and so given unconditional value to all human life and activity.'
- *The previous week* members of the group need to be asked to bring a piece of music, a poem, a picture, a small sculpture, a piece of pottery, a passage from a book, etc., which has particular meaning and beauty for them. It doesn't need to be a 'religious' item. Creativity is a divine gift and doesn't need an extra layer of religious legitimacy. These items are now shown, played and shared with a short introduction about why the item has been selected, and maybe a short time to respond. This activity will consume most of the time available in the session.

Way through

God is the Creator and we are made in God's image. When we create we are therefore co-creators with God. For some the arts are thus a doorway to faith, while for others they remain simply an alternative. Is there anything we can do to help people see the divine origin of their creativity and that of others? Or is it like colour-blindness: some see it, some don't?

Way forward

Is there any artistic activity (and let's include gardening, cooking and other 'normal' creative activities) which members of the group want to develop? How can the group encourage each other in this?

Deeper

Find a picture of Rembrandt's *Return of the Prodigal Son* or a small copy for each member of the group. Ask them to think where they would place themselves in the picture and why. This could be shared (but not discussed) in the group, and then silence given for personal reflection and prayer. Music (possibly Arvo Pärt) could be played quietly as background.

Collect

Faithful Lord
whose steadfast love never ceases
and whose mercies never come to an end:
grant us the grace to trust you
and to receive the gifts of your love
new every morning
in Jesus Christ our Lord.

The Lord's Prayer: possible variations here include group members saying the prayer in any other language in which they are proficient, or a sung version can be used, or one played on CD.

V. Let us bless the Lord. R. Thanks be to God.

Jesus – in a world of faiths

Anchor passage: John 14.1–10

Way in

- Read the anchor passage and keep a full minute's silence to reflect on it.
- What contact have you had with members of another faith? Have you experienced their worship, and if so, how did you feel about it?

Way through

- *Anchor passage*: John 14.1–10. Divide the group into three, with each sub-group taking one of the three positions outlined on page 121 – the exclusivist, pluralist or inclusivist. Take verse 6 of the passage and discuss how you understand that verse from your adopted position, challenging each other – politely, of course! – as you see fit.
- Does the logos concept (p. 122) seem a fruitful way forward or does it compromise the uniqueness of Christ?
- What is it about Jesus that you would point to as most significant, in a conversation with a believer of another faith?
- What does 'evangelism' mean in this interfaith context, and how could you envisage it proceeding?

Way forward

Which, if any, of the dialogues described on p. 123 do you think your church might enter? With whom would that be, and what would be the next step?

Deeper

Place a large candle in the middle of the group and alongside it put a picture or pictures of members of other faiths (available on the internet if necessary), either at prayer or not. Invite members of the group to pray silently, or aloud if they want, asking for or offering whatever seems right to them. The way of praying and the things prayed for will come out of the particular style of discussion that has just taken place.

Collect

Eternal Lord
our beginning and our end:
bring us with the whole creation
to your glory, hidden through past ages
and made known
in Jesus Christ our Lord.

The Lord's Prayer

V. Let us bless the Lord. R. Thanks be to God.

Jesus – to the end of time

Anchor passage: Ephesians 1.3–10

Way in

- Read the anchor passage (slowly – it's rich and complex), and keep a full minute's silence for reflection.
- Are you worried about the future? If so, what about, and for whom?

Way through

- Is the Christian faith offered or received as 'a great counter-cultural narrative' in our society (p. 130), or is it just another narrative but with 'religion' bolted on? Why is this (whichever it is)?
- 'We will need to leave behind our tribal loyalties to the parti-cular banners of church tradition and theological preference that we habitually wave at one another. We will have instead to declare simply that we are "followers of Jesus" (p. 132). Is that possible?
- What do you make of the 'second coming' of Christ? Literal, metaphorical, spiritual, or what?
- *Anchor passage*: Ephesians 1.3–10. 'A plan for the fullness of time, to gather up all things in him [Christ].' Is this a helpful image for the final purpose of God, and the way it will be?

Way forward

'A Jesus man [or woman]' (p. 136). How has this study course helped you to be that kind of person?

Deeper

If the group is brave enough, sing a hymn or modern song that focuses on Jesus. Possible ones would be: 'At the name of Jesus', 'Lord Jesus Christ', 'There is a redeemer', 'How sweet the name of Jesus sounds', 'Christ be our light' (Bernadette Farrell), 'Shine, Jesus, shine', 'Jesus is King and I will extol him', 'Jesus is Lord, creation's voice proclaims it', 'Crown him with many crowns', 'What a friend we have in Jesus'.

Collect

Almighty God
in Christ you make all things new:
transform the poverty of our nature by the riches of your
   grace
and in the renewal of our lives
make known your heavenly glory;
through Jesus Christ our Lord.

The Lord's Prayer

Sing another hymn or song!

V. Let us bless the Lord. R. Thanks be to God.

Notes

A word at the beginning

1 Liam Gallagher, *Times Magazine*, 8 August 2009.
2 'A light in the darkness', *Times 2*, October 2004.
3 Albert Schweitzer, *The Quest of the Historical Jesus* (London: Macmillan, 1956), p. 403.
4 Philip Yancey, *The Jesus I Never Knew* (Basingstoke: Marshall Pickering, 1995), p. 15.

1 Jesus – a personal obsession

1 Gerard Hughes, *God of Surprises* (London: DLT, 1985), p. 36.
2 Brian McLaren, *A Generous Orthodoxy* (Grand Rapids, Michigan: Zondervan, 2004), p. 333.
3 Dietrich Bonhoeffer, *The Cost of Discipleship* (London: Macmillan, 1963), p. 99.
4 Matt Ritchie, blog, *Running with the Lion*, September 2007, <http://mattritchie.wordpress.com/2007/09/>.

2 Jesus – the magnificent outsider

1 Michael Paul Gallagher, *Dive Deeper: The Human Poetry of Faith* (London: DLT, 2001), p. 125.
2 Gerald O'Collins, *Jesus: A Portrait* (London: DLT, 2008), p. 1.
3 St Augustine, *Enarrationes in Psalmos*, 44.3.
4 I am indebted for the following approach to Palestinian society to Brian McLaren, *Everything Must Change* (Nashville, Tennessee: Thomas Nelson, 2007), Chapter 6.
5 Alison Morgan, *The Wild Gospel* (Oxford: Monarch, 2004), p. 79.
6 Terry Eagleton, 'Lunging, flailing, mispunching', *London Review of Books*, 19 October 2006.
7 List suggested in Peter Walker, *In the Steps of Jesus* (Oxford: Lion, 2006), p. 72.
8 Robert Farrer Capon, *The Mystery of Christ – And Why We Don't Get It* (Grand Rapids, Michigan: Eerdmans, 1993).

9 Tom Wright, *Matthew for Everyone* (London: SPCK, 2002), p. 36.
10 Herbert McCabe, source untraced.
11 Austin Farrer, source untraced.
12 David Day, *Pearl Beyond Price* (London: HarperCollins, 2001), p. 73.
13 Morgan, *Wild Gospel*, p. 114.
14 David Scott, *Church Times*, Good Friday, 9 April 2004.
15 Rob Bell, *Velvet Elvis* (Grand Rapids, Michigan: Zondervan, 2005), p. 20.

3 Jesus – centre point of history

1 Quotes taken from the internet.
2 Libby Purves, *Holy Smoke* (London: Hodder & Stoughton, 1998), p. 182.
3 Hugh Rayment-Pickard, 'Time', in John Bowden (ed.), *Christianity: The Complete Guide* (London: Continuum, 2005), p. 1195.
4 Rayment-Pickard, 'Time', p. 1196.
5 Lesslie Newbigin, source untraced.
6 Told in Timothy Radcliffe, *What is the Point of Being a Christian?* (London: Burns and Oates, 2005), p. 31.

4 Jesus – changing the rules

1 Tim Butcher, *Blood River* (London: Vintage, 2008).
2 Simon Jenkins, *The Guardian*, 2 May 2008.
3 Matthew Parris, *The Times*, 27 December 2008.
4 Sermon quoted in Philip Yancey, *Soul Survivor* (London: Hodder & Stoughton, 2001), p. 20.
5 Timothy Radcliffe, *What is the Point of Being a Christian?* (London: Burns and Oates, 2005), pp. 2, 4.

5 Jesus – the world's hope

1 Brian McLaren, *Everything Must Change* (Nashville, Tennessee: Thomas Nelson, 2007).
2 Dietrich Bonhoeffer, *Ethics* (London: Macmillan, 1965), Introduction.
3 Zygmunt Bauman, *Globalization: The Human Consequences* (London: Polity Press, 1998), p. 75.
4 Joel Bakan, DVD, *The Corporation* (Zeitgeist Films, 2003).
5 Timothy Radcliffe, *What is the Point of Being a Christian?* (London: Burns and Oates, 2005), p. 155.

6 Bono, from <www.brainyquote.com/quotes/bono>.

7 See <oneworld.net/article/view/144146/1/3319>.

8 McLaren, *Everything Must Change*, p. 233.

9 McLaren, *Everything Must Change*, p. 165.

10 McLaren, *Everything Must Change*, p. 240.

11 G. K. Chesterton, *What's Wrong with the World*, Ch. 5, <http://www.gutenberg.org/etext/1717>.

12 Told in Peter Price, *Undersong: Listening to the Soul* (London: DLT, 2002), p. 106.

13 McLaren, *Everything Must Change*, p. 171.

14 <www.thinkexist.com>.

15 Martin Luther King, *Strength to Love* (London: HarperCollins, 1963).

16 Quoted in McLaren, *Everything Must Change*, p. 126.

17 Matthew 6.33.

6 Jesus – crazy about the Church

1 Rowan Williams, *Tokens of Trust* (Canterbury: Canterbury Press, 2007), p. 112.

2 Timothy Radcliffe, *What is the Point of Being a Christian?* (London: Burns and Oates, 2005), p. 22.

3 Gavin White, *The Mother Church Your Mother Never Told You Of* (London: SCM, 1993).

4 Thomas Merton, source untraced.

5 Timothy Radcliffe, *Seven Last Words* (London: Burns and Oates, 2004), p. 44.

6 Buzz Aldrin, source untraced.

7 Gregory Dix, *The Shape of the Liturgy* (1945, new edition London: Continuum, 2005).

8 *Church Times*, 14 August 2009.

7 Jesus – partner in prayer

1 Lord Hailsham, *The Door Wherein I Went* (London: Collins, 1975), pp. 54–5.

2 Louis de Bernières, *Captain Corelli's Mandolin* (London: Minerva, 1995).

3 Henri Nouwen, *Sabbatical Journey* (Fort Collins, Colorado: Crossroads Press, 1998).

4 'The secret life of Mother Teresa', *Time Magazine*, 3 September 2007.

5 Martin Laird, *Into the Silent Land* (London: DLT, 2006), p. 15.
6 Brother Lawrence, *The Practice of the Presence of God*, numerous editions.
7 Elizabeth Barrett Browning, from *Aurora Leigh*, Book VII.1, <http://digital.library.upenn.edu/women/barrett/aurora/aurora.html>.
8 <http://www.langhampartnership.org/2007/08/06/john-stott-address-at-keswick/>.
9 George Herbert, from *The Temple*, <http://www.luminarium.org/sevenlit/herbert/prayer1.htm>.

8 Jesus – in a world of pain

1 Elie Wiesel, *Night* (London: Bantam, 1960), p. 62.
2 C. S. Lewis, *The Four Loves* (1971, new edition London: HarperCollins, 2002).
3 Richard Coles, from a broadcast talk reprinted in *Independent on Sunday*, 6 March 1994.
4 François Mauriac, foreword to Wiesel, *Night*, pp. x–xi.
5 J. K. Rowling, *Harry Potter and the Philosopher's Stone* (London: Bloomsbury, 1997).
6 Kate Atkinson, *When Will There Be Good News?* (London: Doubleday, 2008).
7 Rowan Williams, *Tokens of Trust* (Norwich: Canterbury Press, 2007), p. 88.
8 Fyodor Dostoevsky, *The Brothers Karamazov* (Oxford: Oxford World's Classics, 1994).
9 George Carey, *Know the Truth* (London: HarperCollins, 2004), p. 366.
10 Sheila Hollins, source untraced.
11 Dennis Lennon, *Turning the Diamond* (London: SPCK, 2002), p. 22.

9 Jesus – in the mind of the artist

1 Emily Dickinson, from 'Tell all the truth but tell it slant', in *Complete Poems of Emily Dickinson* (London: Faber & Faber, 1976).
2 Neil MacGregor, source untraced.
3 Richard Dawkins in a series of debates organized by the Science Network at the Salk Institute, California, November 2006.
4 Quoted in R. F. Holland, *Against Empiricism: On Education, Epistemology, and Value* (Oxford: Basil Blackwell, 1980).
5 Gustave Flaubert, *Madame Bovary* (London: Bantam Classics, 1982).

6 Quoted in Bel Mooney, *Devout Sceptics* (London: Hodder & Stoughton, 2003), p. 8.

7 Colin McGinn, writing in *The Times* (date unknown).

8 Harvey Cox, *The Seduction of the Spirit* (London: Simon and Schuster, 1973).

9 Article in *Sunday Times* (date unknown).

10 Jesus – in a world of faiths

1 Geoffrey Parrinder, *Jesus in the Qur'an* (London: Sheldon Press, 1965), p. 16.

2 Quoted in M. M. Thomas, *The Acknowledged Christ of the Indian Renaissance* (London: SCM Press, 1969), p. 9.

3 Mahatma Gandhi, *The Message of Jesus Christ* (Bombay: Bharatiya Vidya Bhavan, 1940), Preface.

4 Mahatma Gandhi, *What Jesus Means to Me* (Ahmedabad: Navajivan Publishing, 1959), p. 18.

5 Geza Vermes, *Jesus the Jew* (London: SCM Press, 2001); *The Passion* (Harmondsworth: Penguin, 2006); *The Nativity* (London: Doubleday, 2007); *The Resurrection* (London: Doubleday, 2008).

6 Quoted in W. Jacob, *Christianity through Jewish Eyes* (Cincinnati, Ohio: Hebrew Union College Press, 1974), p. 17.

7 In Channel 4 programme *Revelations*, 16 August 2009.

8 Austin Farrer, source untraced.

11 Jesus – to the end of time

1 John Mortimer, letter to the *Daily Telegraph*, 28 April 1999.

2 Tony Blair, *New Statesman*, March 2009.

3 Andrew Motion, *The Guardian*, 17 February 2009.

4 *The Week*, November 2007.

5 Spike Milligan in John Pepper, *The Good God Guide* (Westbury: Eagle, 2002), Foreword.